Young at Art

Young at Art is a practical guide to playbuilding for teachers working with students at an upper primary and secondary level. Focusing on an area often neglected in traditional drama textbooks, the book covers the process of devising drama, and the teacher's role in facilitating students collectively to become playwrights, actors, designers, directors and critics of their ensemble work. The playbuilding process is covered in a structured manner, which includes:

- **Mapping the territory**: identifying critical issues relating to teaching and learning in playbuilding, and laying the basic foundations of understandings and practice.
- **Levels at work**: offering three approaches to playbuilding, catering for a range of learning experiences.
- **Playbuilding for all**: exploring theatre practitioners' techniques, working with students' personal stories and narratives and playbuilding with a contemporary edge.

An essential guide for all drama teachers, *Young at Art* covers practical teaching issues and strategies for working with groups of students to help them perform their playbuilt stories to an audience, as well as techniques for student assessment and evaluation, providing a wealth of exemplary starting points and approaches. The book offers detailed guidance on working with students to help facilitate the collaborative creative and reflective processes, offering practical ideas and structures which can be easily implemented in the classroom.

Christine Hatton is a drama educator, researcher and consultant who has worked in schools, systems and universities in Australia, the UK and Singapore.

Sarah Lovesy is an educational drama consultant, and over the past twenty years has worked extensively with pupils as a drama teacher in schools and as a lecturer, teaching undergraduate and postgraduate students to become drama teachers.

Young at Art

Classroom playbuilding in practice

Christine Hatton and Sarah Lovesy

Routledge
Taylor & Francis Group

LONDON AND NEW YORK

First published 2009
by Routledge
2 Park Square, Milton Park, Abingdon, Oxon, OX14 4RN

Simultaneously published in the USA and Canada
by Routledge
270 Madison Avenue, New York, NY 10016

*Taylor & Francis is an imprint of the Taylor and Francis Group,
an informa business*

© 2009 Christine Hatton and Sarah Lovesy

Typeset in Bembo by RefineCatch Limited, Bungay, Suffolk
Printed and bound in Great Britain by
TJ International Ltd, Padstow, Cornwall

British Library Cataloguing in Publication Data
A catalogue record for this book is available from the British Library

Library of Congress Cataloging in Publication Data
Hatton, Christine, 1965–.
   Young at art: classroom playbuilding in practice / Christine Hatton and
Sarah Lovesy.
      p. cm.
1. Improvisation (Acting) – Study and teaching (Secondary)
2. Playwriting – Study and teaching (Secondary)   I. Lovesy, Sarah, 1950–.
II. Title.
   PN2071.15H28 2008.
   792.071'2–dc22   2008012660

ISBN10: 0–415–45478–6 (pbk)
ISBN10: 0–203–89072–8 (ebk)

ISBN13: 978–0–415–45478–0 (pbk)
ISBN13: 978–0–203–89072–1 (ebk)

Contents

Acknowledgements

We would like to thank our families for their support while we were writing this book. We also wish to acknowledge that the drama strategies presented in this book are ones that we have created ourselves as well as ones that we have elaborated upon from our collegial associations. Finally, we would like to thank the many drama students who have shared their group stories with us in our playbuilding classrooms and who made this book possible.

Welcome to our book

Young at Art is a practical guide to playbuilding for secondary and middle-school drama teachers and their students. It is a book focused entirely on the practice of playbuilding inside the classroom. It offers a wide array of ideas and different types of playbuilding projects for teachers and students of varying levels of experience. It addresses key play-building issues that arise from *the floor* and offers teachers effective strategies for successful teaching, assessment and evaluation of classroom playbuilding processes.

Most drama curriculum frameworks and syllabuses around the world have *playbuilding* as a central focus. Other terms are used such as *devising drama/performance* or *collective creation*. In most drama curriculum materials in schools the process of students making their own plays is revisited frequently as they progress through their years of drama learning. Despite being such a central part of curriculum documents there are few texts that directly unpack the teaching and learning process of playbuilding in the classroom, nor are there dedicated texts that offer detailed examples of scope and sequencing play-building processes. Approaches to playbuilding are not entirely uniform across schools, systems and countries. Drama teachers' work contexts, curriculum demands and teacher training experiences vary widely within individual countries and across the world. This book gives detailed accounts of playbuilding practice, offering teachers models and ideas for providing young people with exciting and rich learning opportunities in the classroom.

Young at Art is a text written by teachers for teachers and as such, it is mindful of the demands of daily drama teaching and the many educational and personal benefits drama learning provides for young people. A key feature of the text is its unique and distinctive approach to playbuilding, where teachers are offered various ways of working with students of differing levels of experience in playbuilding: beginner, intermediate and experienced playbuilders.

Overview of the book

This book is structured to cater for different contexts, ages and levels of playbuilding experience. It offers a range of processes and starting points for playbuilding as well as offering models for working with particular types of playbuilders. Learner profiles are offered for each type of playbuilding group and there is a real consideration of the particularity of their learning needs as each chapter unfolds. This differentiated model allows teachers to see the kinds of strategies to be used and shows how they may extend each group to move beyond what they already know or what they can do. The book is separated out into three parts for ease of use.

Part I Mapping the territory

Chapters 1, 2 and 3 unpack many of the critical issues relating to teaching and learning in playbuilding such as laying the basic foundations of understandings and practices; issues the teacher must consider such as their role in the creative process, planning and assessment, issues of audience; creating positive climates for playbuilding, leading the learning; organisational issues and problems as well as ways of evaluating the teaching process.

Part II Levels at work

Chapters 4, 5 and 6 offer three approaches to playbuilding: theme-based, character-based and location-based playbuilding for the different types of learners: Beginner (*Level 1*), Intermediate (*Level 2*) and Experienced (*Level 3*) playbuilders. These chapters provide specific models for teachers to use and experiment within the classroom. The teaching strategies scaffold within this framework and therefore they represent a progression of teaching and learning. Each section of the chapters is a discrete unit of work but teachers can also use segments from each section to create their own unit of work if that is more suitable for their particular students.

The teaching strategies suggested in these chapters could be taught at different levels of learning depending on the maturity and age of the students. Students could easily be beginner playbuilders at 12 to 13, or aged 16 to 18. The age and stage of students may not always match their level of playbuilding experience. Therefore we have constructed the chapters to allow for flexibility of approach and student skills.

Part III Playbuilding for all

Chapters 7, 8 and 9 offer ways of working that can be used with all types of students, and teachers can adapt these to suit their needs and contexts. These three chapters capture new, inventive and proven approaches to playbuilding, providing teachers with guidance and processes to playbuild using ideas that interest students in the twenty-first century, such as integrating prominent theatre practitioners' practices into their plays, working with students' personal stories and narratives and playbuilding with a contemporary edge.

Part I

Mapping the territory

Chapter 1

Playbuilding at the centre of classroom drama

PLAYBUILDING IN CONTEXT

Playbuilding is a dramatic art form with its own established set of structural principles which require students collectively to become the playwrights, directors, actors, designers, and critics of their ensemble work. The playbuilt or devised work is created from scratch. It is an original work derived in the main from those who participate in the creation of it. These participants collaborate to fashion out a play through experimenting and critically shaping a whole piece of dramatic art. The starting points and creative processes used in playbuilding are varied, experimental and because they result from collaborative art making, playbuilt works are by nature, multiple in perspective, multi-layered in nature and multi-vocal in the sense that they represent a collective composition of stories, ideas and images drawn from the particular group of devisers. There is not one preferred way or approach taken to playbuilding in schools nor in theatre companies that create devised theatre.

Playbuilding or devised drama is not a new concept when you consider that people have collaboratively devised or created theatre throughout history. There are many theatre companies past and present who devise or make their own plays, creating work from the collaboration of artists for particular purposes and contexts. (Note: for an excellent discussion of devising in theatre see Oddey [1994] and more recently Heddon and Milling's work [2006].) Indeed it is possible to trace processes of devising in various theatre forms, histories and cultural contexts around the world. In theatre, *devising* work tends to imply collaborative creative processes where participants contribute equally and freely to shape the work. Often this approach is seen as more democratic in nature and community oriented, sometimes in opposition to the more hierarchical, text-driven nature of mainstream or commercially oriented theatre. Alison Oddey characterises devised work in terms of its creative freedoms and also its social purpose in communicating shared ideas and meanings. For Oddey 'the process of devising is about the fragmentary experience of understanding ourselves, our culture, and the world we inhabit' (Oddey 1994, p.1). Her notion of devised theatre, drawn from her analysis of a range of companies and practitioners, is one of collective meaning making that is shaped *through* the creative process of making a play. Certainly this idea of devising as a way of making meaning is one that is firmly embedded in school-based playbuilding practice.

Heddon and Milling (2006) question the assumption that devised theatre is an inherently non-hierarchical, collaborative practice. For them, the ideal of true democratic collaboration is questionable when looking at theatre companies with strong directorial leadership and work that also includes text-based plays. They provide an interesting map of the rhetoric that frames devised theatre as:

> a social expression of non-hierarchical possibilities; a model of co-operative and non-hierarchical collaboration; an ensemble; a collective; a practical expression of political and ideological commitment; a means of taking control of work and operating autonomously; a de-commodification of art; a commitment to total community; a commitment to total art; the negating of the gap between art and life; the erasure of the gap between spectator and performer; a distrust of words; the embodiment of the death of the author; a means to reflect contemporary social reality; a means to incite social change; an escape from theatrical conventions; a challenge for theatremakers; a challenge for spectators; an expressive, creative language; innovative; risky; inventive; spontaneous, experimental; non-literary.
>
> (Heddon and Milling 2006, p.5)

There are a number of threads here that would resonate for drama educators as they use playbuilding to give students access to the art form as participants/artists, makers of meaning and culturally aware and critical citizens. Many of these ideals and approaches are evident in the playbuilding processes of the classroom.

PLAYBUILDING AT THE HEART OF CLASSROOM DRAMA

Across the world playbuilding or devising is a key element of drama curriculum documents and mandated syllabuses. While its focus, terminology and importance varies from country to country, most drama curriculum makers see playbuilding or students making original drama works as a central and critical aspect of drama education. Such a view is underpinned by the belief that if students are to understand the art form they need to learn to play with it and manipulate it in innovative ways that communicate ideas and representations about their particular lives, stories and worlds. As students progress through their drama studies at school they learn how to craft their dramas in more independent and complex ways. The prevalence of playbuilding in so many drama curriculum materials highlights the central place it has in the subject. Such a positioning reflects the pedagogical belief in the importance of young people's art making in drama and the primacy of experiential, enactive learning.

As a genre and methodology of educational drama, playbuilding is connected but quite different to the genre of process drama in the sense that the creative process is tailored to make an art work – a play, usually for an audience. The positioning of teachers and students at various stages of the creative process is quite different to process drama where students learn from their improvised experiences within the fictional contexts being explored and their finished work lacks a separate audience. In playbuilding students craft their own drama art works by improvising, experimenting and shaping the final work, usually to be shared in a performance. In playbuilding students have a clear sense of their own roles as dramatists and as players as they collaborate and develop the work into its final form. In playbuilding processes students continually step in and out of the work, reflecting on its development as a coherent piece or dramatic statement as it grows. They explicitly consider the impact of the work and the relationship they wish to create with their audience; they have to ask continually what they want to communicate to the audience, and how they would like to communicate it.

Playbuilding processes usually last several weeks and large-scale playbuilding projects can even take months, particularly if students are creating their work for particular audiences and occasions, such as festivals or performance tours or assessments. In a playbuilding framework, processes and performances are equally valid, and can be equally valued depending on the given circumstances.

PLAYBUILDING IN THE CURRICULUM

The place of playbuilding inside the curriculum and the way in which it is conceived varies across education systems and contexts. A quick glance at some of the drama curriculum models and syllabuses around the world give an impression of how playbuilding is currently defined, positioned and learned in schools. If we look to some of the drama examination syllabuses in secondary schools in various countries we see student playbuilding as a core genre and process; one in which students are able to demonstrate their skills and knowledge about the art form. For example, in the UK, the Edexcel GCSE and AS/A Level Drama syllabus offers devised performance as examination options for students. In this option students are assessed on their abilities to take on roles, use their expressive skills, connect with other performers on stage and their audience, convey and control the style and form of their piece, and show a good understanding of the content and purpose of their drama.

In Australia playbuilding features prominently in drama syllabus documents in all states. For example, in New South Wales it is the core drama form set for study throughout all the years of schooling (K–12). As students complete the final years of their drama studies, they:

> learn to collaborate in devising original presentations using dramatic elements, structures and performance styles. Students learn how to use acting skills and performance spaces and how to establish an actor-audience relationship appropriate to style and purpose.
>
> (NSW Office of the Board of Studies, Stage 6 Drama Syllabus 1992, p.17)

Similarly in British Columbia, Canada junior and senior secondary drama students learn how to create dramas, select appropriate dramatic forms for representing particular ideas and experiences (8 to 10: Ministry of Education, Province of British Columbia 1995, p.50). They 'engage in the creative process (exploration, selection, combination, refinement, and reflection) to create theatre works' (11 to 12: Ministry of Education, Province of British Columbia 2002, p.13) and 'learn how artistic components affect meaning in theatre works, and how to manipulate these components to achieve specific purposes or effects' (11 to 12: Ministry of Education, Province of British Columbia 2002, p.14).

In New York, a core strand of the drama curriculum involves students creating, performing and participating in drama. In Grades 9 to 12 students:

create and perform theatre pieces as well as improvisational drama. They will understand and use the basic elements of theatre in their characterizations, improvisations,
and play writing.

(New York State Education Department 2004, p.40)

Students devising their own dramas is a key area of both classroom study and practice.

This brief glance at the positioning of playbuilding in drama curriculum documents
around the world suggests that drama teachers need to be expert in playbuilding processes
and competent in leading the learning process as students make their plays. This text offers
teachers detailed guidance and ideas that will enhance their leadership of playbuilding
processes in the classroom.

THE PLAYBUILDING PROCESS

The playbuilding process encourages a cooperative approach to exploring the world
through enactment and the collaborative nature of playbuilding enables students, in their
groups, to engage in a creative process of sharing, developing and expressing ideas. Playbuilding is interactive and draws out imagination and creativity in a group; the essence of
playbuilding is for the groups to explore ways for their ideas to be reinvented, to be fresh
and new, or perhaps challenging. During the playbuilding process students often take a
starting point (such as a topic, theme or pretext), then they improvise, discuss and explore
ideas and styles in action using the elements of drama, reflect on the work as it takes shape
and then select and structure the work into play form. In doing so, they utilise their
existing knowledge of the elements and conventions of drama to make a dramatic product:
a play. They negotiate with others to create the work at every stage. Throughout the
learning process the teacher's role swings from leading the playmaking to acting as a guide
on the side, facilitating the way the students negotiate the devising process and create their
work.

Figure 1.1 provides an overview of the key elements and creative processes involved in a
playbuilding project, many of which occur in an integrated fashion over time.

In playbuilding reflection is a continuous practice as students juggle the emerging
themes, characters and dramatic elements within the work. In drama, the core practices of
making, performing and *reflecting* the elements of drama are integrated as the work takes
shape. In devising drama and in learning in drama the teacher uses a careful balance of
structure through dramatic conventions and constraints in order to open up the work
for collaborative creation. The drama experience for participants thrives on the right
mix of controls and protections and the way the form and process open up possibilities
and ambiguities (Simons 1997). During this process both the teacher and the students
participate in the meaning making and shaping of the work.

Like the devising ideals listed by Heddon and Milling (2006), classroom playbuilding
operates on less hierarchical relationships between students and their drama teacher.
Rather than working as a director in playbuilding the teacher shares the authority and
often defers responsibility for the work as it takes shape. The teacher works to create those
moments and contexts where students' ideas and art making practices in drama offer them
rich and challenging occasions for learning.

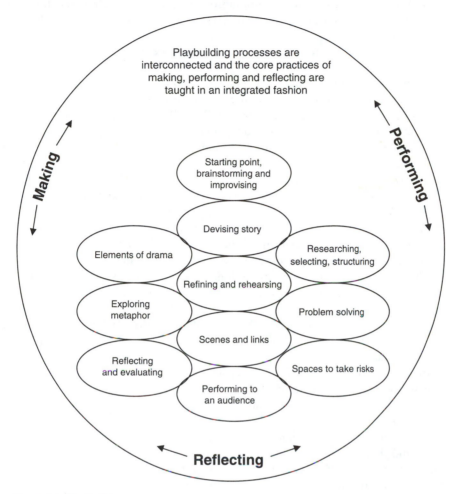

Figure 1.1 Playbuilding processes

LEARNING IN AND THROUGH PLAYBUILDING

In this book we articulate how a scaffolding environment provides opportunities for meaning making and learning for participants (Lovesy 2003; Hatton 2004a). Playbuilders learn through immersing themselves in the creation of their own group stories. While doing this they learn about their expressive and creative skills as key instruments in the processes and final performances of their projects. During a playbuilding project the students build creative relationships with each other through managing and solving personal and artistic problems and through their group's ongoing collaborative experiences they learn to rely upon and trust their collective drama wisdom.

Many theorists in educational drama have tried to articulate how drama provides opportunities for meaning making and learning for participants (Bolton 1979, 1986, 1992). Much of what has been written and researched, however, explores drama learning in relation to process drama and the immersion of students in role-based learning in improvised work. Even though playbuilding is a significantly different methodology, student learning through role-play, engaging with the aesthetic of the art form and the ways in which they make meanings from their engagement in the dramatic process, is the same.

Playbuilding is the interplay between the actual and the fictitious in the drama class-room and drama and theatre educators use the term *metaxis* to describe this type of learning (Lovesy 2003; Hatton 2004a). Burton (1991), O'Toole (1992) and Carroll (1996) have all referred to Augusto Boal's notion (1995) of *metaxis* being at the heart of the transformative learning in drama education and in playbuilding. *Metaxis* is a mental attitude, a way of holding two worlds in mind, the real and the dramatic fiction simultaneously, by the participant in the drama frame (Carroll 1988). *Metaxis* is like the *subtexts* of the playbuilding class, where words, images, ideas, knowledge, physicality, feelings, conscious and unconscious imaginings occur concurrently. This process of *metaxis* enables playbuilders to identify with an array of situations and roles and, through their identification and interpretation of the drama, students find their attitudes and perceptions changed by the experience. *Metaxis* enables students to engage in the *make believe* of dramatic playbuilding contexts and links to what Vygotsky referred to as the dual effect of play. It is the interaction of the real and fictional that generates the learning for students as they work through their playbuilding. They learn as they craft scenes that allow them to walk in someone else's shoes. In this way, the playbuilding can provide the aesthetic space for challenging ideas and practices and can offer students new ways of knowing, seeing and being.

The imaginative act of drama learning enables both a representation of real life and a transformation of it within the dramatic activity. Burton (1991, p.9) sees the drama process as a means of transforming reality into discovery. Figure 1.2 offers a useful way of conceptualizing the process.

Essentially the identification generated through playbuilding enables participants to make discoveries and draw meanings significant for them and their community. The enactive and negotiated nature of playbuilding is perhaps the most exciting for drama students, their teachers and researchers. Learning in playbuilding is both lived and performed, as fiction and as a fictional version of life. The embodied symbolic representation of playbuilding invites students to engage with fictionalised dramatic contexts and to craft their own fictional worlds, thus enabling students

> to both think and feel as another person, to experience a range of cognitive and affective states not directly accessible to him or her. It involves an extension of the participant's perception of the world and his or her experience of it.
>
> (Burton 1991, p.18)

In the collective experience in playbuilding, layers of meanings operate within the fictional and real worlds at play during the dramatic process. Therefore the capacity of students to hold two worlds simultaneously in their minds and bodies in the playbuilding classroom implies that *metaxis* is occurring all the time; it underplays the work being carried out by everyone in the class.

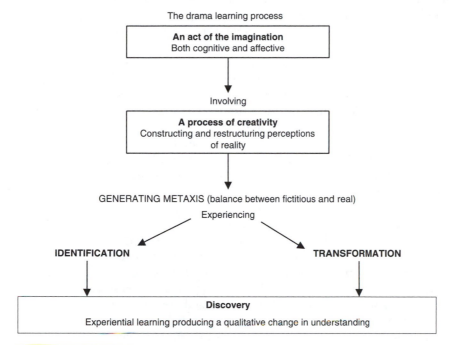

Figure 1.2 The drama learning process

BEING YOUNG AT ART IN THE TWENTY-FIRST CENTURY

As teachers construct the processes and pedagogical architecture (Zatzman 2003) for students to make drama and make meanings from their devised plays, it is important for teachers to be mindful of and responsive to the climate or context the work is created in. During the process of playbuilding students exercise their expressive skills, their negotiation skills, their understandings of dramatic structures and elements and their sense of stagecraft. They also learn about themselves and others quite profoundly as they shape their drama works. In terms of learning, students learn by playful immersion and engagement with the creative collaborative playbuilding process, but in order to do so they draw from the bank of their own knowledge and experience to create and inhabit the stories and action onstage. Each playbuilding process and product reflects the group's skills and knowledge of both drama and living at any given time. The more skilled the group in terms of drama knowledge, experience and expressive skills, the more polished the play they produce. This does not mean that the work of skilled students has necessarily more resonance, dramatic effect and significance than more inexperienced students. It simply means that the theatrical tools and expertise they have available to them differ and also that differences in age/stage and life experience will throw up different challenges for the teacher.

In secondary school contexts playbuilding processes often open up ideas or stories that hold particular significance for the group who are devising the work. Often the drama work captures and frames the concerns or problems of particular groups and school communities. The play the students make at any given time is a reflection of them, their worlds and concerns at that moment. Because of this, teachers can often re-use or re-visit ideas and strategies, yet each group will interpret and create their own work in their own unique way. While the time and context informing the playbuilding processes of young people offer wonderful opportunities to explore the ways in which art mediates culture and informs meaning making, this contextual grounding of young people's art works also presents many challenges for the teacher. These challenges are pedagogical, ethical, political and artistic. A number of these are discussed in Chapters 2 and 3 and also throughout the remaining chapters of this book.

At the time of writing this book, young people are living and learning in interesting times. The impact of technologies and globalisation on education, experience and lifestyle is unprecedented. In a more participatory, playful world of immersive digital technologies, old certainties, storylines and methods of teaching, learning and living are becoming increasingly inadequate to cater for twenty-first century learners. Young people are already learning, playing and living with technologies as active participants, players and content creators. They are the *click and go* generation. They edit, sample and appropriate material from everywhere, often with a less than critical lens. They interact and perform selves and virtual identities alongside peers they may not like or contacts they may never meet. They participate, play and record life as it happens and then share it with others on social networking sites. They write blogs, fictions and use forms of communication that reduce interactions to mere acronyms. Relationships can be conducted and ended via *sms*. Technology has seen a rise in relational shorthand via SMS and MSN alongside the highly public and not always honest presentation of self via *MySpace* and *Facebook, YouTube* and other forms of posting self online. Young people experience identities, communities, connection and sadly, social alienation, in ways that their teachers and parents have never known. Opportunities for thinking things through, questioning what you make and do, making decisions, experiencing roles and relationships live, face to face and unmediated are becoming increasingly rare or altered.

Playbuilding with twenty-first century learners has to account for this highly media-savvy, performance-aware generation. This means more than merely infusing performances or playbuilding processes with technologies as tools. Playbuilding processes must engage with the technologies but also the immersive technology-rich worlds, stories and lived experiences of students. Students' drama processes and works become important opportunities for making connections, understanding ourselves in context and in relationship with our world. Chapter 9 provides teachers with possible ways to engage students when playbuilding in this digital age. We hope teachers and students find the ideas and structures in this text useful in inspiring a whole range of exciting playbuilding projects *on the floor* in the drama classroom.

Chapter 2

Teaching and learning issues

CONSIDERING THE ROLE OF THE TEACHER IN THE CREATIVE PROCESS

In playbuilding the teacher plays a variety of roles within the process as a whole in order to create rich contexts and opportunities for learning. In general terms, the teacher considers the quality of the devising process overall and provides key steps and strategies to move the group forward in their art making and also in their skills and understandings. Drama teachers should have a clear sense of the playbuilding process in mind as they lead the learning. They will have structured the experience for students so that their ideas can take shape in dramatic form in clear phases of the process. The level of deliberate leadership of the teacher depends largely on the teaching context and the level of playbuilding experience of the class. This does not imply that teachers lead any less with more experienced playbuilders, rather the way they lead caters for more student independence and higher levels of skill and knowledge.

When considering their role within the playbuilding process, drama teachers might wish to consider the way they:

- *Initiate the work* – How will it start? What are the ground rules? What activities will kickstart the creative process?
- *Engage students in experimentation and improvisation* – What strategies, when? How do you invite students to experiment in practical embodied ways?
- *Encourage the group to collaborate effectively* – How do you organise the groups? How do they work at each phase? How do you monitor them as they work? When do you intervene when a group is experiencing difficulties? How do you intervene and support them? How do you facilitate respectful peer relations as the work develops?
- *Invite students to reflect on their ideas as they take shape* – What key questions or interventions? When? What forms will these reflections take? How are the insights fed back into the work?
- *Select and use language to lead, critique and support the work* – How do you affirm and critique/support students as artists and individuals as well as encourage divergent thinking and dramatic risk taking?

Other teaching considerations particular to playbuilding are discussed throughout the remaining chapters of this book, in relation to each specific unit of work and student group.

Even though playbuilding is a collective enterprise it is important that the teacher maintains a sense of leadership of the group, while also balancing the needs of the group's collaborative process. The drama teacher needs to have leadership of the learning process, however, in playbuilding authority and authorship is given over to the students, with the teacher acting as a more expert playbuilder/artist and a guide on the side. In this sense, the teacher's *leadership* within the playbuilding process is particularly complex and challenging, because it is a mix of providing the necessary constraints and structures for students to create within/against, while at the same time providing a sense of safety and openness, so that the group can freely experiment and take creative risks on the floor. This requires a kind of *leaderly practice* that Brad Haseman (2002) has described for process drama, but his ideas can also be applied to the teacher's role within the playbuilding process, as Figure 2.1 shows.

- Leading the activities, moving the group from discussion, to improvisation, through devising and reflection as the work takes shape.
- Listening and building upon the students' comments in group work, extending the boundaries of their creative process with suggestions, avenues for exploration, questions just at the right time.
- Helping the group to see connections/make links to give the scene work shape within the emerging whole work, making links between ideas and fragments of stories or symbolic representations.
- Picking up on the nuances of their engagement, what they laugh at or enjoy, what they feel is dangerous or difficult terrain. Intervening gently or directly as the situation requires.
- Understanding the power dynamics within the group, who speaks and how, who listens and attends. Noticing who is silent and why . . . monitoring how this affects the collaborative creative process and role taking.
- Keeping tabs on the way small group work is developing, guiding the work towards originality and fresh interpretation.
- Moving students through the structured creative process, allowing time for play, engagement and reflection.
- Saying less at critical times when understanding is emerging, withholding the answers or intentions of the drama activities so that participants can meet them spontaneously, openly and honestly.
- Shaping the consensus of the group, finding ways to weave together different views, ideas and stories to form a coherent symbolic shape.
- Being attentive to each participant and the way they are making sense of their drama experiences by listening, observing them in action, prompting, questioning, side-coaching, protecting, cajoling, noticing/praising small steps and gains as they unfold in the work.

(Hatton 2004a and 2006)

Figure 2.1 Leaderly drama teacher of playbuilding

The teacher needs to work intuitively and creatively as they lead the students' playbuilding processes. In practical terms this means a heightened level of attentiveness to emerging ideas and representations and also clearly evident interest in how the students are travelling at any given point in the devising process. It is important for teachers to remember they are facilitating students' creative development as artists and as people. In playbuilding, teachers need to notice any gains made and attend to these gains as they arise. Good drama teachers structure into their playbuilding lessons deliberate ways to check in on the emerging understandings and the work as it happens in process, for example through providing cycles of sharing and evaluation at key intervals.

Another issue particular to playbuilding is the teacher's need to focus on achieving learning outcomes and targets alongside the desire to disperse their authority over the content and form of the work. Playbuilding is truly a student-centred learning process, where the ideas and the art work are derived from the students. Teachers need to resist overt theatre directing so that the students *do not lose their ownership of the work* and their independent creative expression. For the work to be a true reflection of the group, it is important that the teacher has a creative approach to the playbuilding and lets the work take its own shape. Students can sometimes resent teachers trying to skew the work in a particular direction or style that reflects their tastes and ideas rather than those of the students making the work.

Drama teaching practice and playbuilding as a key form within it challenge teachers in ways quite unlike other areas of the curriculum. Drama educators work in intensely collaborative, relational ways in the classroom as they lead and work alongside their students. The *ethic of care* (Noddings and Witherell 1991) necessary for good empathic teaching (Arnold 2005) is particularly heightened in the drama classroom, where students are collectively creating, improvising and sharing ideas in practical and embodied ways. Effective drama teachers have good interpersonal skills and can read the dynamics of the group at work as it happens. They set up structures and ways of working that are founded on principles of inclusion, respect and participation. Students need to negotiate and create their drama work in a classroom climate of safety and trust. Good drama teachers work actively to facilitate this and strive to help the group to collaborate effectively.

PLANNING FOR RICH LEARNING

Planning and programming for successful playbuilding involves teachers considering at length the way the playbuilding projects fit into their given curriculum documents and their requirements and how they fit into their programme of drama learning as a whole. In some countries the prescribed drama subject curriculum (i.e. syllabuses and frameworks) explicitly lay out what must be taught, how and when and how it should be assessed or examined. The term *curriculum* refers to all the planned learnings offered by the school (Print 1993, p. 3). Teachers know, however, that curriculum is more than simply delivering content and implementing the syllabus. Curriculum is a broad term that can be interpreted quite differently around the world. Print (1993, pp. 5–6) offers some broad ways to characterise the idea of curriculum:

- curriculum as subject matter – a body of content to be taught;
- curriculum as experience – a set of broad experiences across schooling;

- curriculum as intention – planned and prescribed, e.g. outcomes;
- curriculum as cultural reproduction – reflecting and reinforcing culture;
- curriculum as *currere* – the running of the race/a lived experience.

Drama teachers will notice as they look through different syllabuses from around the world that the interpretation of curriculum and indeed drama curriculum can differ profoundly from state to state, country to country. Teachers interpret the subject curriculum in quite different ways, to suit their particular school contexts. They may plan for a whole series of topics, processes and forms, but there is much they do in the classroom that extends beyond the curriculum as planned and into the hidden curriculum. Drama contributes significantly and positively to the way students experience their schooling and often provides social and critical learnings that last beyond the drama lesson or project. Current research in drama education points to the way drama curriculum as planned can also contribute significantly to a whole range of unplanned outcomes that form part of the hidden curriculum in school (see Hatton 2001, 2002, 2003, 2004a, 2004b, 2004c, 2006; Sallis 2004; Gallagher 2007). This is addressed in this book as we discuss issues of student collaboration and exploration in their playbuilding.

When creating units of work teachers need to consult their system requirements, subject curriculum documents, and their school policies. Today's teachers participate more than ever in the process of making decisions around curriculum as *implementers, adapters, developers* and *researchers* (Print 1993, p.17). Curriculum planning can take place in a number of ways as teachers make decisions around *what* is worth learning (what knowledge?), *how* (processes of learning and instruction) and *when* (sequencing). A number of countries have moved to using the backward planning model of curriculum planning (Wiggins and McTighe 2001) where teachers start at the end of the learning process at the point of the desired results (outcomes), then plan the acceptable evidence (assessment) to be collected and then design the learning experiences (activities and strategies) that will provide that evidence.

In playbuilding teachers will have a clear sense of the end point of the learning and what they want students to gain in terms of knowledge and skills as they work through the creative process. Often the end point involves a demonstration of the process in the form of a performance or sharing of the work. Drama students will frequently have outcomes to achieve relating to each of the core practices of drama – *making, performing* and *reflecting on the drama*. This means that teachers will need to consider and assess how these outcomes are addressed in all phases of the work, such as the experimental phases as well as the performance and evaluative phases.

Drama education and playbuilding are both grounded in constructivist approaches to education. Drama learning is an intensely social process where the learner cooperates with others to create the work and invests in the process. As a consequence, students' ownership of the learning and sense of empowerment grows as their expertise in the art form and playbuilding develops with experience. The teacher's role is to engage students as they create their drama works, encouraging them to experiment with ideas and draw their own meanings from the work. In the playbuilding process the teacher and the other students collaborate to extend each learner and the shifting of ideas in action and in discussion, providing learners with ways of thinking and doing drama beyond their level of expertise. In this sense the playbuilding process actively builds the students' zone of proximal development (Vygotsky 1978). Often the teacher builds into the playbuilding process opportunities for students to learn from each other, and test out their ideas for a critical audience of teacher and peers.

Drama and playbuilding are often taught in mixed-ability classrooms. This book offers teachers various approaches to playbuilding in terms of student experience; however, most classrooms have learners of different needs which need to be addressed. Teachers can adapt the units and approaches here to take in a wider variety of needs such as literacy and language development, social, conceptual, mobility, giftedness and others. Group-devised work thrives on student difference, with each learner being responsible for their own roles and ideas and overall contribution to the work. In this sense good playbuilding processes enable all students to participate in ways that best suit their interests and abilities. The important notion for students to understand is that diversity and difference actually makes for a far richer drama process and product as students learn to work with those differences in creative ways.

ASSESSING PLAYBUILDING

Each of the units presented in this book offer different ways for teachers to assess the drama learning (formative and summative methods). A range of strategies are used and criteria for each assessment strategy are tailored to suit the type of playbuilding process and the level of experience of the students. Students are assessed individually and/or in groups and there are strategies for self- and peer assessment. We have not given any indication if the assessments should be graded, marked or ranked as this is the prerogative of each school and their country's governing educational bodies.

Assessment fosters understanding which leads to deeper playbuilding knowledge. An innovative assessment can also provide motivation to achieve at the highest possible standard of learning and to help solve a group's dramatic problems. Assessment occurs as a regular part of teaching in playbuilding as it enhances learning and recognises that learners use their current understanding to discover, construct and incorporate new skills and knowledge into their project. There are two types of assessment processes:

1   Assessment *for* learning is concerned with assessing the ways in which the group, and the individual students within it, learn. It is more often than not teacher assisted, and has an emphasis on the students' and groups' potential for change to help expand the learning. Students can be put under a great deal of pressure if they feel they are continually being assessed so they do not need to know generally that an assessment *for* learning activity is occurring; it must always be remembered that this is the teacher's monitoring tool and any activity should be seamlessly integrated into the process work.

2   Assessment *of* learning comes at the end of the process when the teacher judges the work using a given set of criteria, and adheres to the mandatory assessment requirements of a given drama syllabus. Implicit in assessment *of* learning is that the work is complete, and that there can be no further opportunity to help the students and the groups in this project. In this end assessment the criteria are usually applied to each individual student, rather than to the group, as this is often a mandated requirement by educational examination boards. It is important to remember that in assessment *of*

learning the teacher will keep in mind the students' strengths and weaknesses when planning the next unit of drama work.

Feedback on assessment tasks is important. Teacher feedback can vary along the lines of explanation, interpretation, application, and/or group knowledge. Teacher or peer feedback, given in an empathic and insightful manner, enables the groups to expand their knowledge and problem-solve dramatic dilemmas. Feedback can open up the play-builders' imaginations and should be based on:

- teacher and peer openness;
- teacher sensitivity to group feelings;
- teacher receptiveness to the group's learning.

Assessment is there to help students to take responsibility for themselves, their thinking and their actions, as well as a diagnostic tool for the teacher.

PLAYBUILDING PRODUCTS AND AUDIENCES

As teachers lead playbuilding processes in the classroom it is important to be mindful of the way each activity and step in the creative process contributes to the final piece and also for whom the work is intended. Careful consideration needs to be given to the potential audience of the work. Teachers will need to consider the students' levels of skill and experience and what type of performance situation the students might be ready for. It is important particularly for beginner playbuilders that their confidence in making and performing their own plays is given time and space to grow. Each student needs to experience success in their playbuilding activities. Teachers need to ensure students perform in an atmosphere of safety and trust, where the students' work can be performed and received in a supportive environment. For this reason, beginner playbuilders in par-ticular need to feel protected in the performance process as well, either by performing as part of the whole-class play, or for smaller audiences where there is perceived to be less personal risk to the individual. Teachers should also consider the important learning that can take place when students are their own audience (class as audience) and build in reflective activities to maximise these opportunities for learning.

If students' playbuilding work is performed for audiences beyond the classroom, such as other classes, or parents or communities, it is wise to factor this into the process of devising the work. This enables the students to actively take on board the needs, tastes and concerns of their audiences and refine their work according to their purpose, performance context and their intended impact. Sometimes it is important to explain to audiences prior to performance what the playbuilding process has involved and how the work has grown from the group experimentation in the classroom. This is critical because audiences often do not have an understanding of the way playbuilt work takes shape in schools, nor do they understand that it is a collective enterprise.

It is a good idea to involve the students as dramatists explaining their work and briefing their audiences, to give their audience an insight into the creative process that led to that particular dramatic product. Depending on the age and sophistication of the playbuilders, teachers need to consider the suitability of the work for particular audiences. Young people will often want to address controversial issues through their playbuilding processes, which in turn means careful consideration of *who* the audience will be. Drama teachers often need to mediate between student-created work and the potential audience. This can sometimes be a difficult task as teachers balance the needs and wishes of students alongside community and public tastes. Good drama teachers invite students as dramatists to engage in the process of cultural dialogue as they consider their playbuilding products and its potential impact. The public and live nature of drama performance in schools presents particular ethical and pedagogical issues for drama educators.

INTEGRATING THE CORE PRACTICES: MAKING, PERFORMING, REFLECTING

Classroom drama learning is characterised by three core and integrated practices: making drama, performing drama and reflecting upon the drama:

- *Making the drama* refers to the students participating in the development and exploration of creating fictional situations. They learn the importance of collaborative ensemble processes.
- *Performing the drama* refers to students demonstrating performance skills, knowledge and understanding appropriate to the style of the playbuilding, and actively being introduced to the dynamics of a variety of actor–audience relationships.
- *Reflecting on the drama* refers to students critically appreciating the effectiveness of their making and performing and synthesising their collective devised drama knowledge. In playbuilding students reflect continuously on the work as it emerges.

Different curriculum documents around the world will sometimes use other terms to name the basic practices that describe the learning process. Whatever the terminology used, it is important that teachers understand that these are linked or interconnected activities, each informing the other throughout the creative process of art making in drama. *As such, these are taught in an integrated fashion rather than a linear way.* This book illustrates how teachers might do this in practice.

Throughout a playbuilding process students should have various opportunities to make, perform and reflect on their work as it evolves. In this sense students are gaining valuable experience in these practices as they shape their work. Students soon learn that a strong critical creative process yields strong dramatic products. In playbuilding, processes and products are inherently connected. These practices become more complex as students' knowledge and skills in art making increases. As students become more expert dramatists they learn to create work that is more challenging, innovative and critical in its content, form and style and they engage in these practices in more dynamic ways.

CREATING COLLABORATIVELY

Group work is integral to playbuilding, and group work in playbuilding is about students' bodies and minds actively engaging with the real and imaginary worlds around them. Playbuilding groups are made up of all kinds of individuals; this ensures diversity. The diversity of a group is an important factor in helping the group to generate ideas because each student brings their own unique imagination to the project, which then merges into a unique group imagination.

Students engaged in devising playbuilding can be thought of as an integrated group of young people developing their own social and cultural interactions, while simultaneously creating their own theatre production; this process is a creative experience where everyone is actively involved in every learning experience. During this process the students have to be guided in how to co-exist so that each individual student can be a productive group member. And it is in this environment that the teacher takes responsibility for their playbuilders' learning through planning dynamic teaching strategies which inspire their students to reach and extend their potential.

Collaboration and commitment to a project is essential to playbuilders' relational group work, and teaching to foster this is embedded in all the strategies discussed in this book. Collaborating is a process that involves every student taking responsibility for the group's work which means they must learn to respect each others' ideas and understand that all group members' ideas are a creative step in the making and performing of a playbuilding project. During this process the students discover that when a group collaborates they can take dramatic risks and creativity flows. Of course sometimes young people find it hard to collaborate and commit to a project; when this occurs the teacher can implement a classroom management contract for the disruptive behaviour. This can include an individual work contract, which discusses areas the student feels happy about, areas they are experiencing difficulties with, areas in which they wish to improve, and ways in which they wish their teacher could help them to improve; this type of contract can be mutually drawn up and can also be a contract for a group experiencing difficulties. So a fundamental pedagogy in playbuilding is about commitment to the project and collaborating imaginatively and creatively with other students in a variety of group playbuilding projects.

In any type and level of playbuilding, groups are formed and reformed, and while forming groups the teacher needs to take into account group size, friendships within the group, the emotional relations between the members, learning styles, skills of the students and the proposed teaching strategies. The teacher has the responsibility to create different groupings for different playbuilding projects, so that they provide a continuous and evolving learning environment for their groups.

The teacher could form:

- groups that are randomly selected so that the students learn to work with and respect students they may not have worked with before;
- mixed-ability groups which broaden students' skills, knowledge and understanding of a variety of peer dramatic approaches;
- skills ability groups which allow students the opportunity to work with peers of similar creative intelligence;
- part friendship groups where students can feel safe and secure working with a friend(s) while simultaneously learning to work with others;
- small groups of 3–5 where students have the capacity to work intimately with their peers;
- larger groups of 6–12 where students work with a wide range of peers while learning about different approaches to a project;

- groups by interest in a particular playbuilding topic;
- whole-class group-based playbuilding, where students negotiate a broader range of ideas and dramatic possibilities. When students work as a whole class the teacher is often leading the learning more overtly during the creative process.

Each of these different group structures is about interacting. Individual members of a group do not work in isolation, and interacting entwines the group members in their common project. Each time a student joins a different group they have an expectation of how that group will develop its playbuilding from their prior knowledge of the class or their own experiences. The group in turn has to identify, respect and merge these different skills, knowledge and understanding while emotionally relating to each other in an integrated manner. Therefore each of these different group structures is about the complex process of *listening, interacting* and *creating* with different people, and it is important for the teacher to think carefully about group composition which will enable ideas to flourish within a project. In the units of work in our book we have given a variety of suggestions about different groups' sizes for different types and levels of playbuilding projects.

The next chapter discusses how to teach playbuilding creatively and gives practical examples to help the teacher begin the process.

Chapter 3

Teaching playbuilding creatively

CREATING AN OPEN SPACE FOR DISCUSSION

Classroom drama relies on students participating voluntarily in the work. Students cannot be forced to *do drama*. If there is no dramatic contract in place, where the students agree to participate in the creative work, experiment dramatically and suspend their disbelief to engage in the exploration of fictional contexts and characters, then the drama work cannot happen.

It is important to explicitly introduce the concept of playbuilding to students as they begin to learn how to playbuild and then to reiterate playbuilding's function and purpose every time any playbuilding project begins. For example, the teacher could ask level 1 playbuilders:

What is playbuilding?

- A dramatic form, genre or way of working in drama?
- A creative and collaborative process of building and making an original play?
- Ensemble work where ideas, decision making and experimenting are done as a group?
- A teaching strategy that demonstrates the collaborative and ensemble nature of the roles in playbuilding?

or they could pose questions for any level to discuss:

- What are the differences between devising a drama through playbuilding and exploring scripted drama?
- What roles would students need to take on if they were devising a playbuilding project?
- Who takes them on and why is this important?
- What kind of skills and ground rules would be necessary to ensure a good creative process?
- Why do we playbuild?

Participation in playbuilding is active, where students create the work and take responsibility for its content and its form as well as communicating it to an audience. The starting point for the students' playbuilding is therefore very important, and it can be chosen by the teacher, or in collaboration with the students. A great deal of thought must be given to this choice as the starting point is the springboard for the playbuilders to create their own stories. All the examples of starting points we have given have been tried and tested on the classroom floor, but sometimes, in a playbuilding project, a starting point that suits one class or one year group may not suit another. A good starting point should give the playbuilders multiple creative paths to travel down so that each group's different abilities and interests can be addressed. For example, teachers may wish to explore any of these ideas as a dramatic entry into the playbuilding process.

Artworks	Movement	Poems
Cartoons	Music	Prose
Concepts	Newspaper articles	Stories
Films and video	Objects	Themes
Internet	People's lives	Topics
Issues	Plays	

Figure 3.1 Starting points

For students to engage in the playbuilding process the teacher needs to plan overtly for the way discussion and participation happen in the creative process. Often drama classrooms provide a window onto the dynamics of friendship groups and power relations within the broader school student population. Drama teachers need to be aware of these dynamics so that they can provide alternatives and possibilities for students so that they learn to collaborate effectively and comfortably for the sake of their drama work. To achieve this often relies on teachers employing specific strategies within the playbuilding process to enhance the social cohesion of the group and create an open space where students can discuss their own and each other's work as it develops. The teaching approaches in our book model overt ways in which teachers can achieve this open space successfully in their classrooms.

One example is the talking circle. The concept of the talking circle is adapted from indigenous cultures that use this communication strategy to hold cooperative and quality meetings for specific purposes (Pór 2006). The talking circle differs from general discussion in playbuilding as its specific purpose is for the teacher to make sure, in a formalised manner, that a few students are not inadvertently dominating the work, and that the creative responsibility is shared by all. When the teacher asks the playbuilders to form the talking circle they must be aware that this is a very special occasion where each student can speak his or her playbuilding truth or the teacher can ask specific questions about the process. This truth must never be a negative truth but a truth to help develop honest and effective communication about the playbuilding processes. If the class chooses an object of importance to them at the beginning of the project, this can be used to allow students to speak and discuss how they will manage or solve problems and/or prioritise their work. The object does not go around the circle but to the centre allowing only the students who wish to speak the opportunity to do so while the others remain silent. The talking circle should only be used at pivotal moments in the playbuilding, and students with the teachers can decide when it should be formed. It is everyone's responsibility to be actively listening, respecting the discussion, and planning solutions, but the teacher should take a leaderly role in guiding individual students or groups to the desired outcome.

CONSIDERING THE TEACHER'S USE OF LANGUAGE

Effective drama educators use language expertly to engage students in the enactive learning processes of classroom drama. In particular, good drama teachers know how to select the appropriate language to discuss student work in ways that keep students interested and involved in the drama. Drama teachers know the importance of praise and critique and the impact these have on the emerging creativity and identities of their students. It is critical to drama and to playbuilding that teachers use effective language when:

- initiating the work
- giving clear instructions
- facilitating around the episodes of enactment
- guiding the group when they are at work
- giving feedback to students
- asking questions.

In each of our chapters we have modelled language that scaffolds in difficulty and complexity and this demonstrates how to add depth and breadth to the playbuilder's learning. Through language, teachers support their students and challenge them to try alternatives and to think more deeply about how they work and what risks they might take in their drama work.

Questioning is an area that needs further elaboration. In playbuilding, teachers ask hundreds of questions during every project from simple recall questions to more complex and abstract questions. The ability to ask intelligent and searching questions, to use questions to stimulate playbuilders' imagination and hence their creating is integral to the teaching of playbuilding. Questions are a central part of explanations and explorations and a teacher needs to develop their approach to questioning techniques as well as exploring ways to help their students question their own work so that they can find answers to act upon.

Once a group has decided on a starting point, or been given a starting point to playbuild from, these types of questions can be asked to stimulate ideas (adapted from Weigler 2001):

- What is this about?
- What makes this interesting?
- How will we create a group story from the starting point?
- What else do we need to know?
- Where can we go to get more information?

Questioning is also important during the process of developing scenes where students are layering on dramatic structure, such as time of day or physical surroundings. In this phase a teacher could ask:

- What impact do time of day and the physical surroundings have on your scene?
- How could you make the purpose of these dramatic structures clearer?
- Why is this the most effective solution to the problem?

If the groups were showing their scene in progress to their peers the following questions could be asked of the class who take on the role of the audience:

- Can you tell the group one aspect of their scene that you find really engaging and why you find it engaging?
- How did time of day affect the scene? If the group changes the time of day would this give the scene more dramatic power?
- How did the physical surroundings affect the scene? If the group were to change the physical surroundings to increase the dramatic conflict, what could they do and how could they go about it?
- Why might your suggestions create a deeper dramatic meaning and engage an audience more fully?

It is a good idea to get the students to write these types of questions down in their workbooks so that they can keep referring to them during their process work.

Questions which are structured empathically will achieve the desired outcome of knowing how to help playbuilders go forward, and it is important for a teacher to listen carefully to the answers. Listening to the reasons for decision, the tone of voice that is used by group members, and the emotions behind the answers enables the teacher to act with integrity and creativity in their future planning.

> **Handy hint . . .**
> A useful text to think about your questioning techniques is Norah Morgan's and Juliana Saxton's Asking Better Questions (1994).

METAPHORIC DEVISING

Playbuilders should be given the opportunity to explore their work through metaphor, as metaphor can transform a group's imaginative and creative energies. A metaphor is an active mode through which to experience drama ideas symbolically as it creates a new context and configuration of dramatic meaning for the playbuilders. Through metaphoric devising students can be encouraged to explore information and knowledge creatively, and to highlight or even suppress certain aspects in their play. Hence metaphor allows students to see dramatic ideas in a new light, as metaphors both amplify and diminish the human experience (Blom and Chaplin 1988; Moore and Yamamoto 1988).

It is important to teach students what a dramatic metaphor is (Lovesy 2003), and how to incorporate it into their work so they can find ways to capture the essence of their group stories. The teacher approaches this learning through introducing students to:

- Themes as metaphoric devices. Metaphoric themes enable a group to catch the sense of their group stories. Such themes as *Captain Envy Versus Princess Ego* or the theme *The good ship censorship* can provide deep possibilities for students to learn more about the world around them.

- Characters as metaphoric devices. Metaphoric characterisation enlivens the feelings, thoughts and subtext of a number of characters in the work. For example, in a character-based playbuilding entitled *The Carnival* a leading character could become *Miss Ferris Wheel* who informs and predicts the action of the play or in another character-based playbuilding about *Consumerism* a character could become the *To buy or not to buy genie*.
- Location as a metaphoric device. A metaphoric location can transform the dramatic action of the playbuilding. For example, in a location-based playbuilding entitled *You who live safely* students could set their performance in a circus tent to highlight and underscore the importance of human safety and the futility of war. Or students could choose a location to perform their work in and change this space into a metaphoric celebratory venue of human safety.
- Objects as metaphoric devices. Metaphoric objects can be real or imagined and the objects acquire significance through the semiotics with which they are endowed in the project. For example, in a themed-based playbuilding entitled *Weddings and beyond* the students could used different coloured materials to demonstrate love, the veil, the baby, the husband, the wife, the divorce, or in a theme-based playbuilding entitled *Dreams* students could use different coloured material to demonstrate the surreal characteristics of dreams.
- Verbal imagery in student dialogue and the creation of visual metaphors with their bodies are other interesting metaphoric devices (Lovesy 2005a).

Students experimenting with playbuilding should therefore be given the opportunity to endow their ideas with symbolic and metaphoric life. Metaphoric imaginative thought can provide rich possibilities for learning and opportunities to layer and broaden the inner and outer life of their fictional group work. Group metaphoric devising can capture the mysteries of dramatic meaning so that what the group believes is the essence of their storytelling is brought to life. Metaphor releases creativity because it is multi-sensory; this multi-sensory capacity means that the metaphoric layers in themselves provide substance and meaning to work. If the metaphor is working well for the students, it will crystallise the meaning and illuminate the nuances to themselves and their audience. Students should be encouraged actively to be responsible for their own metaphoric devising but the teacher needs to facilitate this as sometimes students create metaphors that override the group's ideas in the playbuilding, and the metaphor creates a whole different meaning to what the students intended.

THE ELEMENTS OF DRAMA

All drama learning is informed by and shaped by students' understandings of the elements of drama and their skills in using these *on the floor* and in performance. Haseman and O'Toole provide a useful model of the art form and the way its elements convey dramatic meaning:

The human context (situations, roles, relationships) *driven by* dramatic tension *directed by* focus *made explicit in* place[1] & time *through* language & movement *to create* mood & symbols *which together create the whole experience of* dramatic meaning.

(Haseman and O'Toole 1986, p.viii)

When we think about playbuilding processes other elements can be added to this model such as:

- *Audience engagement* which is integral to students understanding the purpose and meaning of their playbuilding project.
- *Characterisation* as there is a need to differentiate between role and character in playbuilding; role work involves students representing and identifying with a particular set of circumstances, whereas characterisation involves students in the process of developing a fully realised character from their role.
- *Dramatic moments* which are fundamental to helping students to understand that a number of moments make up scenes, and each separate moment is pivotal to developing and building the dramatic tension.
- *Student focus* which needs to be continually nurtured and developed throughout every project.

All elements of drama with their associated meaning could be displayed around the drama room during playbuilding projects to allow students the opportunity to actively refer to them during their making, performing and reflecting processes.

As students become more expert dramatists and playbuilders they learn from their embodied experiences and gradually become more adept and independent when using the elements of drama in their work. Whether students are improvising, playbuilding or working with scripted drama, they manipulate these elements for effect and impact, communicating their ideas through their selective use of the various elements.

In playbuilding, students should have a range of different opportunities to play with the elements of drama in different combinations so they can consider the ways in which the elements are working to achieve their dramatic purpose and impact. Different types of playbuilding processes may involve students emphasising particular elements for a specific style or purpose (e.g. a heightened use of symbol in non-realist or abstract forms and styles).

Every activity and playbuilding process should involve students experimenting with the elements in practical ways and also critically reflecting on the way the elements are working at any given point in their drama work. Discussing the elements of drama during the devising process offers opportunities for rich discussion about the art form and the way students are using it. Teachers can focus on the elements of drama in the way they structure activities, as well as self- or peer evaluation processes. This encourages students to develop their critical thinking skills and their ability to respond to the live and dynamic experience of the drama as both a participant and an audience member.

---

1 John O'Toole (1992) refers to place as *location* in his book *The Process of Drama* and sometimes we use this terminology in our units of work. He also describes *location* as a place of special significance and our location-based playbuilding units are based on this premise.

ORGANISATIONAL ISSUES

The playbuilding process, like other processes in drama learning, can be substantially affected by problems associated with organisation, planning and resources. Critical organisation issues that impact the effectiveness of playbuilding projects are described in the following paragraphs.

Time

For many classroom drama teachers time is a luxury resource. In this book we have given an estimated time in weeks that each phase should take and we have based each lesson on 4×50 minute lessons a week, but this may vary for readers enormously depending on their teaching contexts. Teachers should try to allow for as few interruptions as possible to the units, as they are designed as whole processes. If groups have many interruptions to their creative process it becomes difficult to build the work in a sustained manner and give it the creative coherence needed.

Space

Consideration needs to be given to the way the workshop space is configured and used. Are there desks? Is there an open space for improvising? Is there enough space for students to show their work to each other? There may be times when you want students to work at desks, or on computers or experiment in role. Teachers need to consider how the space is to be used in order to help the work to be purposeful at all times. Teachers need to make sure students are visible to them as they work, for duty of care reasons but also so that they can see how well they are completing each task as they progress through each phase of the playbuilding. Other issues such as what surrounds the working space are also important when trying to control sound levels inside the room and also manage any outside noises when you expect students to focus and concentrate.

Resources

Teachers will also need to consider what additional resources are to be used in each phase, such as music, brainstorming paper, pieces of text, whiteboards, fabric, materials and other properties of significance. It is good to think about how these are used within the learning phases and to consider if they are entirely necessary to fuelling the playbuilding process. Sometimes elaborate props, costumes and resources can be a distraction for groups who have difficulty experimenting in role or making decisions. Consideration also needs to be given to what happens to those same resources after the lesson, for example are they stored, re-used, kept present in the space somehow, and if so, why? Managing resources effectively makes lessons run more smoothly and limits the time wasted on gathering and using them once the lessons are under way. It is ideal if properties and resources can be kept inside the room you are working in and are able to be used and stored easily.

Planning units of work

Planning a unit or units of work should be based on the premise that in teaching and learning, change should occur through effective scaffolding. This involves creating playbuilding projects that do not just transmit knowledge, but which provide a greater intensity and richness of learning more likely to enhance knowledge. A unit of work should be meticulously planned and implemented within the framework of:

- student-centred learning;
- the core practices of making, performing and reflecting;
- experiential teaching strategies which have the characteristics of engaging the whole person, cognitively, affectively and physically as an individual and in the group context;
- experimental teaching strategies which have the characteristics of students physicalising their ideas to solve and manage problems, and to actively work together to explore the world through enactment.

If a drama department teaches a number of playbuilding projects within their drama course they should sequence these units of work to ensure that they scaffold upon one another, and plan each unit's teaching strategies to provide a depth and breadth to their students' learning. Each unit of work created must be scrutinised to further ensure that there is pedagogic variety in the content, thus creating more complex units of work that require an inherently higher level of making, performing and reflecting.

> *Handy hint . . .*
> *When talking with students the teacher uses the word 'project' rather than 'unit of work'.*

Phases

In this book the playbuilding process is divided into four major phases:

- *Phase one: Generative phase*
- *Phase two: Constructing phase*
- *Phase three: Structuring phase*
- *Phase four: Performative phase.*

In each unit of work the first phase kickstarts the creative process by introducing conventions and techniques as well as initiating the exploration that will follow. The second phase involves students beginning to make their play. In the third phase students will be developing and linking their scenes and making decisions about dramatic structure. The fourth phase is one where the students are refining, rehearsing and performing their play in front of an audience. *Evaluation and reflection takes place throughout every phase of playbuilding.*

It is important that students feel that the whole process has a definitive shape and that they are moving through the clear phases as their work develops. Sometimes different phases will take longer than we have indicated in our units of work. If the group chooses to dwell on specific ideas or scenes, activities may take longer, but it is important for the teacher to keep the group moving on towards their intended completion. Sometimes groups can try to change scenes and even projects midway or late in the creative process, which can inadvertently slow down the process as a whole. It is important to encourage students to adapt and utilise their ideas, rather than changing them over and over again.

Warm-ups, scenes and linkings

Warm-ups are an excellent way of preparing playbuilders' bodies and minds individually and collectively. Improvised warm-ups realign students with their creative centre. In a whole class warm-up you can have 30 students working together; this means leaving their social structures and personal lives in the playground, and by entering the playing, the playbuilders can find new perceptions and new awareness. Moreover, playing in warm-ups allows students to explore their bodies and voices by having fun while achieving personal interaction. It is through this structured fun that they are at liberty to find out about themselves and their group. Structured fun can release a certain freedom that students would never have tapped into, and from this, the next stepping stone is crafting their intuition, and constructing their own original playbuilding.

Warm-ups are therefore an integral part of the teaching of playbuilding. Warm-ups allow the students' cognitive, affective and physical selves to become engaged with the drama project they are undertaking. Warm-ups should always have a purpose that relates directly to the playbuilding project. For instance, if you are doing a voice warm-up it is important to tell your students why you are doing this, and how this relates to their character or role development, or if you are playing a tag game it is important to explain how the energy generated in this classroom activity can be transferred to a particular scene that may have lost its dramatic energy.

Every class should begin with a warm-up of one kind or another. Warm-ups can be taught in small groups or as a whole class. You must decide what is appropriate for the needs of your class as warm-ups serve different purposes in the playbuilding. You can use:

- icebreaker activities which allow students to explore the dynamics of new students to the class or new ideas in a fun way and through their verbal and physical domains;
- concentration activities that demonstrate to students the importance of focus, self-discipline, and the power of personal thought;
- improvisation activities that help students practise offering and accepting ideas through using verbal and physical offers (ideas) in a range of different groupings. In this way students are practising spontaneous responses but also practising the collaboration and the exploratory playful approach necessary for good playbuilding;
- movement activities which allow students to recognise and explore the importance of their individual and group bodies and extend students' skills in representing ideas in action;
- trust activities that demonstrate to students the importance of collaboration and commitment;
- vocal activities which allow students to recognise and explore the importance of sound and voice and which focus on vocal production, communication and control so that students learn how to use their voices expressively for different purposes;
- games that have an intrinsic purpose in relation to the whole playbuilding process.

- a wide variety of drama activities which demonstrate to students how warm-ups can be integrated into their playbuilding project.

Warm-ups allow the playbuilders to develop group cohesiveness and a sense of complicity, where they learn to negotiate the dramatic moments together as they arise. They provide individuals and the group with self-confidence; they can strengthen powers of concentration and extend the ability to think imaginatively and creatively. They can be used directly in the playbuilding to explore physical and vocal capabilities, and to explore meaning through abstract concepts. They can be used to help groups link their scenes through deconstructing their improvised situations within a given set of guidelines, and every warm-up should have a focus on collaboration and commitment to learning. The fun and energy created in warm-ups must be extended to the learning in the playbuilding project so that students continuously see the connections. In our units of work we have given a limited number of warm-up strategies as every drama teacher has their own range of warm-ups appropriate to their students' needs, but it is important in the early phases of all playbuilding projects to establish core warm-ups using improvisations and expressive skills as this is the basis of good group work.

Scenes in playbuilding are incidents in the story and hence the plotline. Most scenes groups develop will be between 1 and 10 minutes long. In the main the playbuilders develop a scene by:

- the group discussing and improvising what they want in it;
- actively adding research;
- adding pertinent conventions, techniques and performance styles;
- applying drama structures that have been specifically taught within the particular project;
- evaluating how the improvisation is developing into the scene they have mapped out;
- refining the scene and discussing how to make the next scene.

Often, when a scene has been three-quarters developed, playbuilders will leave it for a week or two while they either develop other scenes, make linkings, devise and add metaphors, or go back over how the story, plotline and intended message for their audience is progressing.

Linkings are also a very important aspect of any playbuilding project as they create the dramatic flow between each scene. Linkings are the dramatic device the playbuilders use to create the transitions from scene to scene, and they add complexity and dramatic meaning to the play which in turn engages the given audience. Linkings must be integral to the sense of the scenes and this often means that they cannot be created beforehand but occur through teacher and students' collaborative thought during the playbuilding processes.

Throughout our units of work we have given ideas to help teach linkings, as well as ideas for different types of linkings, but we list below general linking concepts:

- asides
- audience involvement
- elaborating on one aspect of a performance style or technique

- elaboration of drama games and exercises
- entrances and exits
- extending physical and/or verbal offers
- film, video, multimedia technologies
- masks
- movement
- placards
- poems
- props
- quotes
- monologues
- repetition
- songs
- soundscapes
- the elements of drama (individually or combined)
- warm–ups.

Ultimately anything can be used as a linking device that creates and enhances the details of a dramatic structure. It is important for the playbuilders to experiment continually with their linkings to see if these transitions hold true to their concept of their play. This means that the teacher must have a strong knowledge of dramatic structure and a critical eye as to the effectiveness of the linkings the students are exploring.

TEACHING STUDENTS TO REFLECT ON THEIR PLAYBUILDING

It is important to see reflection as an integral part of the overall creative process in each unit of work. It is imperative that teachers and students do not perceive reflection as an add-on to their work on the floor. Everyone needs to understand that good plays do not develop and operate in a vacuum; they are tested and critiqued and opened up to scrutiny, so that critical and sound structural and performance choices can be made. Sometimes inexperienced teachers will mistakenly use written forms such as journaling and writing as the only form of student reflection. In drama, writing about the work is not more important than the practical experience of the learning itself. Reflection can take many different forms and occur as the work evolves rather than at the end of a process. It is important to foster students' critical thinking and reflective skills right from the very beginning of their playbuilding.

Teachers need to value the talk that happens in and around the playmaking and can structure in opportunities for critical discussion and conferencing as ways to develop students' reflective skills. Students should not be penalised for literacy problems when it comes to reflecting on their drama work. Often students can reflect in discussion but need assistance in developing their thoughts and use of drama terminology on paper. This becomes critical for teachers preparing students for examination-level study (Lovesy 2002). It is critical to ensure students' reflection in action and on action on the floor is targeted first and then transferred into written forms, as they learn to write critically about the work and their experiential learning. Weak writers benefit from scaffolded approaches to writing about the drama work and practice around making judgements and providing examples to support their views.

Students should be required to keep workbooks where they write, develop and record their reflections; teachers should consider varying the format of these reflections to target particular skills and ways of reflecting. Students might:

- record what they set out to do;
- describe what happened;
- reflect on their own experiences;
- record their research and investigative processes;
- create a playbuilding blog, where they add their own input and also respond to peers' comments;
- draw, paint and/or sketch their responses.

EVALUATING YOUR TEACHING OF PLAYBUILDING

A reflective approach to playbuilding is also important for the teacher, when evaluating their own practice and its effectiveness. Teachers need to understand how they are serving their students' playbuilding needs, so they can prioritise improvement in their learning. It is important for teachers to pinpoint what to evaluate, and how to identify the strengths and weaknesses of their teaching. There are pedagogic sensitivities to evaluating drama teaching, such as the purpose of evaluation, who judges the evaluation besides the teacher, how the evaluations are to be used within the drama department and school communities and how formalised the processes of evaluation are. There are many pressures affecting drama educators working in schools but honest evaluation of teaching practice is vital to effective teaching.

In playbuilding the evaluation process is continuous for both teachers and students. Evaluation strategies can be integrated into every unit of work and into every phase of learning so that students become successful learners who enjoy learning and make progress and achievements in their playbuilding classes. Effective evaluation strategies help prepare young people for responsible participation in society. The following information gives advice to help drama teachers organise, collect, analyse and evaluate the evidence from their playbuilding teaching so that they can benchmark their students' performances, and if appropriate compare with the best schools. Evaluation is an integral part of the planning and teaching cycle. It is important teachers think about the evaluation strategies they will use while the playbuilding is under way as they plan their units of work. While the playbuilding process is under way, teachers should consider:

- How are the core practices of making, performing and reflecting being taught?
- Was the learning purposeful?
- Did the work cover what was planned?
- What can the students do that they could not previously?
- What do the students know that they did not previously?
- How are they able to transfer their learning to the next phase of learning and devising?

At the end of a playbuilding unit teachers should ask some pivotal questions:

- Was the playbuilding sufficiently student–centred?
- Was the playbuilding appropriate to the students' level of maturity, stage of development, cultural background and previous experience?
- What teaching strategies were being used and were they appropriate?
- Were the assessments appropriate to the students' age range and content of the project?
- How did the students respond to the playbuilding processes and final performances?
- How could this unit of work be improved?
- How will the students apply this learning to another context?

It is really useful for teachers to write their responses to these questions on the outline of the unit of work. This becomes useful data for future planning because the teacher must implement the changes in their future planning and teaching. This means that in the next drama phase of learning, or when teaching the same playbuilding unit of work again to a different cohort, there is a pedagogical emphasis on change and progress in this new learning environment.

The principles and processes of good evaluation practice are implicit in all the units that follow.

Part II

Levels at work

Chapter 4

Level 1: beginner playbuilders

Teaching considerations for beginner playbuilders

The ways in which beginner students are introduced to drama are critical and important for laying the foundations of basic terms, understandings and practices. They will need early experiences that develop their confidence and comfortableness in working together and in dramatic exploration. Teachers need to provide a range of activities that allow students to practise their emerging drama skills and understandings in a safe and trusting learning environment. The way the teacher leads and facilitates at this point is critical to establishing good working practices, a sense of experimentation and strong group cohesion.

It is often best to work as a whole class with beginner playbuilders. A whole-class approach models very directly to students the good critical, collaborative and creative processes which are necessary for playbuilding. Working as a class provides a safe space for learning how to playbuild, but of course there are times when smaller groups may be advisable. Beginning playbuilders generally need more direct leadership and teaching throughout the whole playbuilding process. The teacher continually guides and facilitates beginning playbuilders. This means that the groups slowly build up their drama skills, knowledge and understandings.

Early playbuilding experiences are critical drama learning episodes, which lay the foundations of important skills and understandings. A strong early playbuilding experience should provide learners with an explanation and understanding of the genre of playbuilding as well as an understanding of the elements of drama and how they work in dynamic, live ways onstage. The focus of the learning should be exploring possible ways to experiment practically with ideas generated from the starting point. Students develop their reflective skills in an ongoing manner as the work evolves over time, so they gain a critical awareness of how important their *reflection in* and *on action* is in the creative process of playbuilding.

Learner profile

Students who undertake level 1 playbuilding may have little experience doing experiential classroom drama with a learning focus. They may have some expressive skills but have limited experience of making their own plays in a detailed or sustained manner. They may have limited experience in a range of dramatic processes or forms or styles on the floor and are just beginning to understand the art form, its elements and practices.

THEME-BASED PLAYBUILDING: EXPLORING A THEME

Unit description

This unit is designed to give students a strong and structured introduction to the playbuilding process. The strategies could be applied to a range of possible themes. For this hypothetical playbuilding unit, we will work with the theme *The Departure* as a whole class. Working as a whole class allows the teacher to gradually build skills and understandings that will become foundational to later work. Students who have had no experience in playbuilding find exploring themes accessible because the learning is broken up into achievable episodes. This means that the students don't need advanced skills to dramatically visualise and devise a whole play.

How long?

Five weeks is the maximum amount of time required to introduce playbuilding to beginners, based upon 4 × 50-minute lessons per week. It is important to set achievable time goals for the students.

Phase one: generative phase (about one week)

Selecting a theme

If the group is new to drama learning or new to working with each other the drama teacher might prefer to select the theme for the group to explore. This would ensure the class has clear parameters for working and exploring together and allow the teacher to facilitate the learning in a more controlled or direct way. The teacher would need to:

- ensure that the chosen theme and also the activities set for exploration enabled students to take the ideas up and experiment with them;
- choose an interesting open-ended theme, one that would genuinely interest the group;
- avoid themes that dictate a message or action or prescribe a way of interpreting the theme that is too teacher/adult in orientation, such as *The generation gap* or *Teenage issues*. Students can easily feel patronised and alienated if they do not feel they are active participants in the decision making in the drama.

When the teacher chooses the theme, the students need to understand why and feel assured at the start of the process that what they do with it and how they interpret it will be up to them, part of their collaborative decision making on the floor.

Allowing the students more freedom to choose the starting theme has its pros and cons. If the students select the theme from a list provided by the teacher or from their own brainstorming, they do feel more ownership of the work. Sometimes though, particularly if the group is newly formed, dominant voices in the class can dictate the direction the group takes and the students may choose themes that are potentially problematic, overly challenging or limiting, such as *Youth Suicide, Racial Tensions* or *Drug Abuse*. Issues like these are enormously complex to investigate in both ethical and playbuilding terms. Often such issues are far more difficult to explore dramatically and sensitively than students realise. Also, choosing a problematic theme for the first experience of playbuilding could signal the pattern for future work or limit the creative scope of the group by allowing them to mistakenly think that sensationalism leads to good drama work. Some groups will opt for such themes as a way of challenging the authority of the teachers or testing her or his position within the school in terms of issues of freedom, permissiveness and censorship.

The best way to lead the initial decision making is through whole-class discussion. Give students a list of about five possible themes as starting points for playbuilding. An introductory discussion with beginner playbuilders could be:

> We are going to build a play together as a whole class. Working in this way will help you to understand the way the playbuilding process works and what you need to do to playbuild effectively in drama. It will be very important to listen to each other, give each idea a chance to take shape by experimenting with it, and work together to decide what is the most effective way to represent our ideas in drama form. You will be expected to contribute ideas, to improvise, to structure the drama and refine it. We will be working towards our own one play, but as we start working you will break off into groups and be responsible for different sections of the play. We will be regularly checking in with each other and evaluating the way the work is emerging over the next few weeks.
>
> We need first to decide together which theme we will be investigating in our playbuilding. We need to think about which of these given themes might give us a range of options for investigation. We don't have to take the theme literally. In fact we will probably use it as a jumping-off point in our explorations. We are going to brainstorm, improvise and delve into the theme we choose, so it is important to choose one that sparks interest for most people in the group. Let's look at each theme and discuss each one properly . . .
>
> Let's discuss:
>
> * What does this theme mean to you?
> * What do you/we know about it already?
> * What would we need to know more about in relation to this theme?
> * How does this theme affect your lives?
> * What ideas does this theme generate for you?
> * Does it give us a range of possible ideas or lines of inquiry to work with?
> * Would an audience be interested in seeing a play about this theme? Why?

This discussion should take place as a whole class. That way the teacher can lead and monitor the sense making as it unfolds and also ask further questions to extend the students' contributions. This discussion needs to model good collaborative practice as students voice their opinions and actively listen to each other. At the end of the discussion the class can decide on the theme by narrowing it down to two, then voting on the best option. Or perhaps, as the discussion continues, a clear preference emerges.

It is important for students to feel as though all suggestions have been considered. If some students' choice of theme or ideas were not chosen by the class, the teacher needs to assure the group that they may be used and reworked in the playbuilding at a later point if it suits the work. It is important for students to see that this is only the beginning of the decision-making process and as such the play has yet to be made. Some beginners may find this open-ended approach difficult as they might want to know the outcome or storyline from the start. They may not be used to working in an exploratory and collaborative way. It is important to encourage students to have an open mind and trust that the process will make the play. Keeping the work open early on allows a whole range of creative ideas to emerge and be tested out on the floor.

Improvisation as a starting point

Working as a whole class, students discuss and brainstorm the theme *The Departure* on the board or on paper. Make sure all ideas are heard and noted; try not to judge the ideas that surface in this early phase. Deter students from trying to predict a whole story or scenario at this point as it is also too early. These early ideas can be incredibly useful to return to when groups are stuck or run out of steam midway in the playbuilding process.

Moving into enactment

Possible strategies could be:

- Using the ideas recorded, students can select a few to work with and in small groups they make a moving soundscape and wordscape from their chosen words.
- Students can then create a machine of the theme, at first in small groups, then as a class. Notice what happens when the machines work at different speeds, or operate at different rhythms? Discuss what ideas are being generated from the work.
- Discuss the stories ideas the theme implies (try to think of as many as possible). In small groups students create a tableau that takes up some of the points and ideas raised in discussion. These images are shared and then *read* and interpreted by the class.

What types of groups and why?

More than likely the teacher will not be overly familiar with the beginning playbuilders' abilities and interests as this is their students' initial experience of devising a group play. In this case the teacher could choose random groupings where students learn to work with anyone in the class, or they could choose part friendship groups where students can feel safe and secure while simultaneously learning to work with others. Keep the groups at 4 to 5 students in a group, this will give a range of interests and abilities. The teacher would facilitate a maximum of 6 to 8 groups in total.

Phase two: constructing phase (about two weeks)

At this point in the playbuilding there could be as many as 5 or 6 different groups beginning to work individually on their playbuilding unit of work. To maintain a sense of class cohesion and to introduce new playbuilding strategies to each group it is very important to start the majority of the lessons with whole-class teaching strategies.

Assessment of learning task

As this is an introductory playbuilding unit of work it may not be necessary to have official criteria. Official tasks may be daunting for beginning students, especially when given out early in the process. Any task should be written out in student-friendly language with the criteria subsumed into it. Of course this depends on school assessment and reporting requirements. A sample task could be:

Assessment *of* learning task

Our class is making a play for presentation. Each person in the class will be a part of the creative process. Each student will be asked to:

- contribute ideas in improvisations and discussions;
- construct short scenes that have a clear dramatic structure and use the elements of drama;
- be an active group member in helping to shape the work;
- reflect upon the work as it evolves and take steps to refine it for presentation;
- participate in the performance of the work by taking on roles and enacting scenes.

The work of each group will be woven into a class play based upon the chosen theme. This play will be presented to a selected audience. Throughout the project your teacher will observe you at work and will ask you to reflect on your own contributions and to critique the work of other students.

Time to prepare
Five weeks

Criteria for assessment
You will be assessed on your ability to do all of the following:

Making the drama
- contribute ideas to further the playbuilding;
- listen to others' ideas;
- collaborate effectively with your group members;
- experiment with ideas practically;
- manipulate the elements of drama for effect.

Performing the drama
- communicate ideas in role;
- demonstrate expressive skills in performance;
- use the elements of drama for effect;
- support other actors in the piece.

Reflecting on the drama
- record the ideas and creative process as it develops in your workbook;
- reflect upon the process of creating and performing the drama work;
- evaluate your own contribution to the work;
- evaluate the effectiveness of the work of other students in the class.

Students will be assessed during (assessment *for* learning) and at the end of the playbuilding project (assessment *of* learning). Teachers should give out the assessment *of* learning task early in the project and discuss what students are expected to do over the five weeks. It is important to discuss the idea of the class play as a collective effort, where each part will make up the whole play. Students are to take responsibility for their own scenes and are expected to contribute to the shaping of the play as a whole. Most of the lessons will involve students actively experimenting and appraising their work. Students may be informed about the way the assessment *for* learning task will be conducted and also how the teacher will use other ways to document and assess their contributions and learning achievements. Other ways teachers could collect and record evidence of student learning could be through skills checklists, observational notes as well as other forms of self- and peer assessment. In this framing discussion about assessment the teacher will also need to explain how the workbook is to be completed and how it will feature in the teacher's assessment process.

Devising the first scene

The teacher asks the students to sit in a circle and explains that after the groups are organised each group needs to find a place in the classroom and discuss how they would like to dramatise the chosen theme. Questions to stimulate the devising could be:

- What connotations or images does the theme bring to mind?
- Have you ever had to leave somewhere or someone behind? If so would you be comfortable sharing that story with the group?
- Why would a person make the decision to leave?
- What would they be leaving behind?
- What would they want to find in their new place?
- When is it easy to leave?
- What makes it hard to leave?
- Are there members of your family currently or in the past who have had to leave their country or home? Why? What happened to them?

The teacher reiterates that once ideas start to flow the students need to get up and physicalise and improvise their ideas. The teacher will need to facilitate the process of using any of the ideas generated in this initial discussion for drama purposes. Remind students they are fictionalising or dramatising the idea rather than re-representing a group member's exact story told in this early discussion.

Developing roles

As the work begins to be explored, students will work in broad roles when they improvise at this point in the creative process. Characters which are more detailed and layered take time and experimentation to shape and refine. They should appear thus early in the piece.

Some strategies for developing roles:

- Turn the ideas of the earlier brainstorming into a photograph called 'The Departure'. What could it show? Who would be in it? What does the photograph suggest about roles, relationships, focus and tension, as well as place.
- Add a few short lines of dialogue to the photo. This can be the words the characters say at that point or the thoughts of the characters or what they cannot say to each other at that point.
- Discuss the different choices made by the groups and their effectiveness. Allow the groups to hear from their peers where and when the work is the most dynamic or interesting. Then let them return to the scenes and heighten those elements. Check in again to see if the scenes are stronger.

> **Handy hint . . .**
>
> *It is important that the elements of drama terminology are used and applied in these improvisations.*

Essential questions

- What ideas are starting to emerge in response to the theme?
- Which roles and contexts are we interested in exploring further and why?
- What are the possible directions each group can take now?

Answers can be recorded on butcher's paper or in workbooks. These form a record of the ideas that are beginning to emerge.

When the groups have physicalised some ideas for their initial scene the teacher could explore teaching strategies such as:

- Beginning, middle and end – progressive tableaux to structure the drama. These do not have to be chronological in time.
- Incorporating mime, music and/or neutral mask, if appropriate, to develop their scenes or give symbolic emphasis to the work.
- Introducing some of the elements of drama to help the groups shape and mould their ideas. Beginner playbuilders don't want to be overloaded with technique so it is better to choose a few elements of drama to focus on, though it is likely that the majority of the elements of drama will be present in the playbuilding. Good key elements to focus on would be role, relationship, focus and dramatic tension.
- Developing and extending roles – role of course is a core element of drama and needs special attention to help the beginning playbuilders create roles that are of interest and/or challenging for them. Students could hot seat particular characters to discover further ideas that might give depth and layers to the story.

Devising the next scene

When each group has developed a structured first scene it is a good idea to introduce the fact that they need to create another one. Of course, each group will be at different stages of their devising but with the use of their workbooks they can record, draw and reflect on their first scene as a way of capturing it mid-process. One good way to capture this is to have each group write a synopsis of the work so far or to record it visually as in a diagram or draw it as a storyboard.

All groups should start the development of their next scene at the same time because it provides cohesiveness for the whole class while devising. The teacher discusses with groups that the next scene does not have to flow on from the first as in a traditional play or TV soap. It can be a completely different approach to the theme and cover totally different aspects. Possible directions could be:

- Exploring the backstory . . . what are the reasons for this departure? What is the sequence of events leading to the decision to leave?
- Delve into a particular character's thoughts or dreams or fears at critical times – these could be about the past or about the future or place they are departing to.
- Focus on objects and action . . . what does the character pack and why?

How to teach basic scene links to the whole class

It is best to limit the playbuilders to a few linking strategies to begin with. As they understand more about the concept of linkings, and as they gain more confidence as playbuilders, they will explore different ways to link their scenes. The teacher models the strategies and the whole class explores how linkings work to create a flow between scenes that enhances and connects the scene segments. As the teacher facilitates each group around the room, suggestions for linkages can be given and the group works with these ideas. Then they present to the class and afterwards their peers give them feedback about the effectiveness of the linkages. Possible linkage devices could be:

- a narrator who links one scene to the next;
- a poem (found or written by the group) that links one scene to the next;
- a movement piece that merges one scene into the next;
- using activities learnt from the warm-ups to merge one scene into the next, e.g. soundscapes that delineate the end of one scene and which merge into a soundscape that introduces the other scene.

How do you know what each group is doing?

It is important for the teacher to assess how each group and student is travelling through the playbuilding by seamlessly incorporating an assessment *for* learning activity. A self-reflection worksheet would be an easy way for teachers to check on the progress of each student and give some constructive feedback to them that will enhance their learning. A worksheet of this kind could be inserted into the student's workbook as a record of the assessment process. This worksheet would enable them to record their evaluation of the work as well as allow the teacher to give direct feedback to them about their learning process and what they need to continue to work on as it progresses. A possible format for this worksheet is a self-evaluation sheet (see Figure 4.1).

The quick self-assessment sheet will enable teachers to check in on individual students and assess their progress mid-process. Alternatively, teachers can ask each group to present

Name	Agree	Not sure	Disagree
I have contributed well to my group's playbuilding			
I am comfortable in the roles and actions I take on in the piece			
I feel that my ideas are listened to and used in the playbuilding			
Each person is working hard in my group			
We need to develop our ideas further			
We know what we are trying to communicate to an audience in our piece			
Our piece uses the elements of drama in an interesting way			
I feel confident that the work will be effective in performance			
What are the strongest ideas or elements of the work so far?			
What do you think still needs to be done to make the piece stronger?			
Teacher's comment:			

Figure 4.1 Self-evaluation sheet

their work so far to the class and to ask the class to comment on how the work could be made stronger. This would enable the teacher to check in on each group and also give direct feedback and guidance after each presentation.

Asking essential questions and how to answer them practically

Where to now? Some groups will want to explore the linkings, others will want to refine or even further develop their two scenes and then explore linkings. At this point students should not be reinventing large sections of their work or reworking new basic ideas. This is a building phase in the work rather than a forming phase. The teacher helps facilitate this stage by asking essential questions of each group and helping them to solve the issues in a practical way.

Questions to ask the students

As succinctly as possible state what your two scenes say to an audience.

- Decide on two or three areas you would like to improve in each of your scenes. Be specific. How can you dramatically incorporate this improvement into your scene?
- What props and costumes do you need and why?
- Do you need to set the scenes in one place or many places? How does this affect the dramatic action? How will you organise the space?

Phase three: structuring phase (about one week)

Developing basic structure and dramatic coherence

Small-group focus

Ask the students to map the dramatic structure on paper. Is it clear and well structured? Ask the group to consider the way dramatic tension unfolds in their piece as a whole drama. Students should be encouraged to consider the cohesiveness of the work and the way tension is manipulated for effect. It may also be useful for them to list the type of tension at work in their scenes and the ways in which they have focused the work to enhance dramatic tension. (See Haseman and O'Toole's book *Dramawise* (1986) for a useful list of the different types of dramatic tension). In a practical sense the groups need to consider how they would fine-tune or refine their scenes to make them flow and also to give them more impact. Give some class time for this polishing phase, then ask each group to show their whole piece to the class. Class members give a last critique of the work.

Whole-class focus

At this point the class returns to working as a whole group with the teacher leading this last phase of the devising process. Important final tasks at this phase are:

CREATING A DRAMATIC STRUCTURE OR SEQUENCE FOR THE
WHOLE-CLASS PLAY

The class discusses and decides on the sequence of scenes or running order for the play as a whole. Students need to be careful to separate similar scenes, to create an effective whole structure and also to consider the way they want the audience to experience the play as a whole. By negotiation a final order is decided.

CREATING SHORT WHOLE-CLASS SCENES THAT WILL TOP AND TAIL THE PLAY

This requires more input from the teacher to lead this discussion and whole-class experimentation, because the teacher has a greater wealth of theatrical knowledge and experience than the group. One way of giving circularity to the play is to use the same scene to start and end the play. It is desirable to have the whole class on stage for the beginning and end of the play as it helps the students feel that this is their play. These short scenes or motifs could sum up the types of ideas the whole group has been interested in exploring throughout the project. You may want to return to those initial brainstorming records to reconsider ideas or comments made by students as they began the work.

Some possible ways to top and tail the play *The Departure* could be:

- a movement scene set at an airport, with choreographed whole-class movement using suitcases;
- sound effects or music to bring on the actors in an interesting way;
- lots of different departures done simultaneously, possibly at an airport;
- visual images in montage and voices or soundscapes;
- return to the machine work done earlier in the project;
- choral work . . . using a poem or a diary entry or letter;
- using a narrator who is a distinctly different character than those used in the scenes, such as an angel of travel . . . a joker or jester . . . or a flight attendant or baggage handler . . . or a personified character such as the suitcase speaks his or her case (pun intended).

CONSIDERING WHAT WILL BE THE LINKAGE DEVICES BETWEEN EACH GROUP'S PRESENTATION

The class will also need to consider how to link each different group's scenes together. An easy way to do this is with music or a sound effect (e.g. a heartbeat, or a clock ticking away or crowd sounds at an airport or train station). The linkage device needs to allow for a smooth transition from one scene to the other in terms of use of space and thematic consistency and it needs to enhance the work as a whole play.

What to do when difficulties arise

The types of difficulties faced by first-time playbuilders are usually ones relating to collaboration, shaping the work and their lack of understanding about how the art form works in action. Here are some suggestions as to how teachers can address these difficulties.

Problems collaborating

Learning to collaborate takes skill, time and trust. The talking circle offers a formalised process for discussing different views. Problems arise when students feel their ideas are not actually used by their group and this could be because the group does not yet have the skills in drama to do the *weaving* of ideas well enough. It is important for the teacher to facilitate and model how this could be done for the group experiencing difficulties.

Sometimes collaboration problems are due to poor dynamics. It is important to remember that trust needs to be built. Sometimes students' peer relationships and power relations guide the group work. The teacher needs to ensure good collaborative practice is both valued and maintained in the playbuilding process. More often than not, poor group work results in a weak piece of drama. Groups need to understand that arguing and wrestling for position merely wastes time and works against the creative process, because people are not supporting each other. Another strategy for groups who *get stuck in a rut* is for the teacher to ask the class to assist the group with ideas about how to synthesise or weave together the different ideas in the group. This reinforces the collective effort required in playbuilding and reminds them of their responsibility to *our play* as a whole.

Problems deciding which ideas/scenes to choose

This is an indication of students' lack of experience with the art form. Perhaps they have never seen a live theatre performance or done drama before. Encourage the students to select the strongest ideas to work with. If students are arguing about the ideas, ask each person to explain the merits of each idea for the success of the piece as a whole. The group could try each idea out practically to see which has more impact, then select the strongest or most interesting options. The students need to understand they must choose ideas that interest the audience, not just themselves. Drama communicates ideas, rather than being a private enterprise.

Lack of stagecraft knowledge and skills

This is a critical one as it impacts the way the work unfolds. It may be important to take some moments out of a few early lessons to introduce some basic concepts about using the space and managing the focus onstage. Short games or activities that could be used as warming-up activities may best teach these strategies quickly. Also useful is to show students pictures of plays in performance and ask them to note the choices made in terms of focus, staging and the actors' positioning on stage and in relation to each other. Of course, the best way to begin this type of learning is to allow the students to see as much live theatre as possible. If you have more experienced students completing projects at the same time, use this beginner group as their audience. Then spend some time discussing the stagecraft at work and the reasons for the choices made.

Problem-managing and -solving strategies

It is important that the teacher guides and models problem managing and solving for the whole class and also for the small groups as they work. This means the teacher needs to be active and mobile in the room, facilitating the drama work as it is emerging, being leaderly (Haseman 2002), but not directing it. The role is more like a guide on the side rather than a directing role. One area of difficulty that arises is that students tend to conflate all their problems together as one big insurmountable problem. It is important that the teacher tries to sort through the crisis and helps the group to tease out what the most critical issues are; only then can they be directly addressed. The teacher can help the group decide a plan of action to address the problems. Sometimes a group which has experienced difficulties needs more time to iron out the problems or needs direct advice about how to work it out systematically and practically.

Phase four: performative phase (about one week)

Refining the play

Allow students time to refine and polish their own sections of the play. Aspects to focus on at this point are:

- smooth linkages and transitions;
- clear roles and relationships;
- control of the stage action and focus;
- establishment and maintenance of dramatic tension;
- decisions about how they enter and exit the space need to be made, particularly now they are part of a whole play.

Students should not be creating new work at this point; rather they should be refining what they already have made.

Rehearsing the play

Rehearsal is the process of practising the piece. If the class is large make sure each group has a chance to rehearse a few times in the space as it will be in performance. Sometimes if beginner playbuilders have been rehearsing elsewhere, like in a corridor or another area, they can get a shock when they have to present in the *real* space. So make sure each group is familiar with the space. Once each group has had their own rehearsal time, return to working as a whole class and do a few run-throughs of the play as a whole. This will uncover any problems with managing the group as a whole, such as where do they go/what do they do when they are offstage?

Performing the play

For beginning playbuilders it is often better that they perform in front of their classmates or in front of an audience that is not too threatening for them. The students' sense of safety and support is important at this critical phase of performing for the first time. If there is another class of the same year that can be invited or a junior class (one year below is ideal) this would be a good first audience. Keep it a relatively small-sized audience. An audience of the performer's friends can be problematic as they can disrupt the work with comments or reactions. Some teachers opt for a *no audience performance*, just for the purposes of assessment. However, it is best practice for students to get a sense of the liveness of performance and the real experience of an audience in the space. This first performance should lay the foundations of skills and understandings as students learn to explore the actor–audience relationship.

Before students perform it is important for the teacher to explain the creative process to the audience and set the expectations in place in terms of how to be a good audience. Many school students have little or no experience of live performance with only screen or mediated performance, hence they do not understand the need to be attentive to and supportive of the actors onstage.

Assessment

Throughout the unit teachers will have various opportunities to make judgements and gather evidence about the student learning that is taking place. This means that a good amount of the work has already been done before the performance itself. It is useful to video these first performances of a class as they make helpful starting points for discussion and reflection afterwards. It is important to remember though, that the video may not be an accurate record of the live performance in itself.

> **Handy hint . . .**
> *It is best practice to gain parental permission before you video students' drama work. Parents also need to know how the video material will be used and stored. Make sure you have other assessment records in case permission is not granted.*

As the students perform their work it helps to have an easily manageable way for the teacher to record their assessment of students' performance skills. Teachers can refashion the assessment criteria into an easy–to–use checklist that enables them to keep watching rather than writing while each group performs.

Evaluation

After the performance of the work it is important to allow the students to discuss the experience of performing and to debrief after the project as a whole. It is important to balance discussion and written evaluation at this point (it should not only be a workbook activity). Allow the students to discuss openly their difficulties and achievements, and to consider what could have been done differently. A good final activity would be to ask each student to set some goals for themselves for future playbuilding in each of the three core practices of *making the drama, performing the drama* and *reflecting on drama*.

CHARACTER-BASED PLAYBUILDING: EXPERIMENTING WITH CHARACTERS

Unit description

In this unit of work students create a range of familiar and unfamiliar characters. They experiment with developing and sustaining a character through voice, movement, belief, and interaction with other characters within a class-devised story. In planning the unit of work the teacher develops strategies that allow all students to create a single detailed character, although sometimes students will also take on varying roles because of the nature of the play they are devising. The playbuilders learn through small scene structures created through the elements of drama. This unit of work is a simple introduction to metaphoric devising; the teacher may not wish to discuss this aspect of learning with the playbuilders, as depending on the maturity of the class, they may think it wise to allow their students freedom in exploring their own group creativity without an overload of pedagogic information.

How long?

Suggested timeline is 5 weeks based on 4 × 50-minute lessons.

Phase one: generative phase (about one week)

In phase one it is important to build on beginner playbuilders' instincts and perceptions of dramatic characterisation as well as their previous skills, knowledge and understanding.

The teacher explains character-based playbuilding to the students:

> In this unit of work you are going to focus on creating a play with strong characters that will be developed from your observations and ideas. Taking on a character means that you develop each character's values and attitudes and their relationships to one another. The questions you need to answer are:
>
> * What interests you about character-based playbuilding?
> * How do you go about developing characters in this project?

The teacher introduces the idea that detailed observation of others is a very important skill in helping to create a character.

Students work in pairs; one of the pair stands to the side of the room and observes their partner's bodily rhythms as they walk. When the observer is ready they imitate their partner. Students swap roles as it is important for everyone to experience this activity. The partners demonstrate to each other their *observation walks*. With the same partner they follow the same structure creating emotional face mirrors. At the end of these activities they discuss how observation helped them to create emotions and rhythms.

From these improvisations discussion takes place about the importance of observation when developing characters.

Building on their observation skills the teacher presents a collage from the *Day in the Life* series of photography books (<http://www.247mediagroup.com/projects/day.html>). These books record the people of a particular country or society over a 24-hour period and have a wealth of interesting photographs. This collage can be of people from one country in different locations or in different countries and locations.

> *Handy hint . . .*
> The Day in the Life *series is created by Rick Smolan and David Elliot Cohen.*

This teaching strategy also introduces a starting point to build the play around. The teacher asks the class:

* Can you describe this person?
* What does this picture tell you all about who they are and how they live?
* How does this person differ to another in the collage?
* What is this person's status? How do you know?

- What do these people have in common and what are their differences and why?
- How could you use this stimulus to build a play from?

The talking circle is formed and every student has an opportunity to say what they think they could playbuild around using this stimulus material as a source of inspiration. A decision may take a few minutes or it may take a couple of lessons. The teacher acts as a guide and a facilitator during this process so that the students do not go off track and are reminded that their playbuilding is to be character-based and therefore they must think about a topic that allows a character's inner and outer life to be presented in their play.

Developing the story

In this hypothetical situation the playbuilders decide that they wish to create a play about *Differences*. Once a decision is made, the whole class, with the teacher, creates a simple story outline about differences. For example, the teacher could take two photographs of different people from the collage and split the class into two asking them to list everything they can think of about that photograph.

When the groups come back together with their findings they discuss and record the differences and similarities in their photographs, which helps them to find a simple storyline to begin their playbuilding. The teacher facilitates this exploration of storyline by guiding it within the structure of the elements of drama. For example:

> Let's imagine that all the photographs you have examined are actually characters who have never met each other but live in a location close to each other. This means that they are in a situation where a story might develop if they were to meet.

The teacher asks the students to follow on from this scenario with *What if* questions. The point of *What if* questions is to build on the story in this scenario as if it was real, and on a stage with characters in action. Every student has the opportunity to pose questions and to answer them but the teacher guides the questions as they need to be focused on the elements of drama (the *elements* covered in each question are italicised) to help the playbuilders to create a simple but effective story.

What if:

- These types of characters came from different villages? (*Characters, situation and relationships*).
- The characters had different characteristics and qualities? (*Characters, situation and relationships*).
- How would these manifest themselves? (*Characters, moment, language and movement*).
- They both wanted something the others had? (*Characters, tension, moment, mood and symbols*).
- Some people from each village tried to get this something? (*Characters, tension, moment, mood, time and location*).
- What would the actions and reactions of the different characters from the different villages be? (*Characters and dramatic meaning*).

- How do all the characters serve these ideas on the stage floor? (*Characters, dramatic meaning and audience engagement*)?

The class is asked to summarise the story that is developing and to write up the outline in their workbooks. For example:

> There are two villages with people who have different ideas and beliefs – scene 1. Perhaps some villagers believe that the grass is greener on the other side – scene 2. One village, or some villagers, try to take over the other village – scene 3. The ending to be decided as we make up our play – scene 4.

Phase two: constructing phase (about two weeks)

In this phase the class makes scenes based on their developing storyline. These scenes are critiqued by one another and recorded in their workbooks. The scenes are enhanced by teaching strategies that are created from the elements of drama. The teaching strategies are given here in a linear fashion but in the classroom they would be sequenced depending on the learning needs of the playbuilders.

Groupings

The class works as a whole group but at times is split into two groups.

Assessment of learning task

The following assessment *of* learning task should be given to the students at the beginning of this phase. It is based on the importance of students reflecting and understanding their play's message and the impact their characters have on this message.

Assessment *of* learning task

The whole class is going to devise a character-based play that will be 10 to 15 minutes long from the starting point of *Differences*. As previously decided by the class the format for your play will be that there are two different villages whose villagers have a conflict of interests. In consultation with your teacher the class will be split in half to create the two villages and each of you will explore and develop a single character.

You will be assessed individually on your ability to:

- develop and sustain your character in the process and final performance;
- collaborate with your peers throughout the project;
- demonstrate that you are totally committed to the project.

In this project it is important to reflect on the message of your character in relationship to the devised play. Your character's message helps to create the overall dramatic meaning and is part of the way the audience is engaged in your play. You need to write (type) up the answers to the following questions in your workbook:

- Why does your character behave as they do in the play?
- What do they learn about themselves and others in the play?

This can be written as a letter, a monologue, a newspaper article or as a reflective statement. It should be 200 to 300 words long and will be handed in a week after the end of the playbuilding project. If you wish you can team up with another student to complete this assessment task, but remember the length of words would double. All points need to be backed up with evidence from the play. For example, you can quote directly from your character or any other characters in the play.

Characters, situation, and relationships

This teaching strategy is based on creating characters that inhabit a society, and the cultures that the inhabitants cherish. The teacher could run warm-up activities that explore the students' own societies, for example the way students' societies are formed and structured, and their different culture traits that are special to them.

The class is split into two villages but they work together to explore what is both similar and different about the two societies they are going to create. This should take no more than a couple of lessons and the class findings are recorded so that everyone has access to the findings. The teacher provides the focus questions:

- How is your society organised? (e.g. do you have different classes of people; upper-, middle-, working-class?).
- What is the relationship between these classes of people? (e.g. do they get on well for the good of the community or not?).
- How is your society governed? (e.g. is it a democracy or is it hierarchical?).
- What are your culture activities? (e.g. do some of you like going to the opera and others to sports events?).
- What traditions (beliefs handed down) does your society hold dear? (e.g. does your society have an annual march to celebrate past heroes or does your society have a holiday festival every year?).
- What customs (particular ways of behaving) does your society hold dear? (e.g. does your society have a particular dance, or ritual they perform?).
- What type of food and drink does your society enjoy? (e.g. does one society drink fruit juices while the other drinks tea?).
- What is it about the people (characters) that inhabit your society that are similar to one another and distinguish them from the other society? (e.g. do you all have a particular way of dressing; do you have particular gestures; do you have particular ways of addressing one another?).
- Name your village (e.g. use a name that reflects your society's attitudes, or create one randomly).

The two villages make up a scene from this information.

Character development

When the students have made decisions about their societies each is asked to fill out a character development worksheet over the coming week. Even though they do this individually they must discuss their developing character with their peers to make sure the dramatic purpose of their character integrates with the story. Remind the students to stick their findings in their workbooks and to fill it out in pencil because as their characters develop they will want to change things.

Name:
Age:
Why is your character in this play? (e.g. their purpose).
What characteristics do you have in common with the other members of your village society?
What is your status in your village society?

External qualities
Background: (e.g. what is your family home like, your education, your hobbies?).
Gestures: (e.g. do you use your hands as you talk, do you shake your head when puzzled?).
Movement: (e.g. do you move with agility, shuffle, stride?).
Posture: (e.g. are you upright, slumped, relaxed?).
Speech: (e.g. do you speak with a coarse voice, a high-pitched voice, a pleasant timbre?).
Props: (e.g. does you character have a personal prop? Perhaps it is a handkerchief, a walking stick, an ipod, a handbag).

Internal qualities
Emotional: (e.g. are you a very emotional character or do you keep your emotions hidden?).
Mental characteristics: (e.g. are you very intelligent, crafty, quick-witted, a bit slow?).
Motivation: (e.g. what motivates you to do what you do; money, family, belief in traditions and customs?).
Spirituality: (e.g. what are your ideals; your religion?).

Characters and their relationships are shaped by the situation
What is the situation in your village?
Because of the situation in your village what are your relationships to the other characters in your society?
What are they with the other village society?

Figure 4.2 Character development worksheet

When they have completed the worksheet the two village groups form a circle and introduce their characters to one another, and from this information they create another scene.

Characters, time and location

The teacher, with the students, creates two village locations on the classroom floor. This is done by each village creating an imaginary location which can be enhanced by other objects such as chairs, tables and/or material. Once this has been completed the teacher asks the villagers to find a space in their location: She or he explains:

> It is 7.30am on a chilly autumn morning and you are going about your morning routine. You need to act and react to the people in your environment, demonstrating some of your internal and external qualities. Think about your status among the other villagers; if you are a high-status character you may use a lot of space; think about how your eyes are an indication of your high status and perhaps you can use them sharply or assuredly to survey the morning scene. Maybe you are a lower-status character so perhaps your body takes up a bit less space, maybe you are a fidgeter, and maybe you find it difficult to look others in the eyes at times, but remember that low-status people are not always timid, they can be very happy individuals, and high-status people are not always stern but can be jovial and good-natured. Experiment with these ideas and take them to the extreme, then draw them back to find out more about your characters in this particular time and location.

The class does the activity twice more, once for midday and once for 10.00 pm. The teacher photographs three moments, one from each *time* improvisation, and projects them onto a screen from which the class analyse how each village's photographs become progressively different due to the change of focus in the characters' relationships. There is also emphasis on the performers' focus which they must have maintained to sustain concentration and belief. From the photographs these types of questions are posed:

- What happened to your characters at different times of the day in the same location?
- Why does time and location affect a character's status?
- What ideas about the story are brought to light because of the improvisations and photographs and how can scenes be made and incorporated into your playbuilding?

Characters, language and movement

The teacher works with the whole class exploring how the different village groups have created the verbal and non-verbal languages of their characters and if they have used detailed movement in their scenes to express the dramatic action. From these explorations the villagers improvise with the energy levels of their character's language and movement. For example, the characters in their village location are asked to remain still, run, stroll, walk, sit down within various timings; added on to this are various sounds that indicate how their characters feel, such as growling, hissing, mumbling, squeaking, shouting, laughing, then silently gesturing, posing, looking, pondering. The two village groups could have a competition that will provide ideas for developing characters' language and movement. For example, the villages hold a race (on chairs, slow motion, three-legged) where the majority of the characters barrack for their village heroes through language and movement. If any of these types of improvisation has potential, the students develop the scene to insert into the storyline.

The teacher sets an assessment *for* learning activity asking each student to create, from their character development worksheet, a 20-second monologue about their purpose in life in this village society. If students need help with *purpose*, give them some examples:

> **Is your character's purpose to demonstrate to the audience that people do care for each other in both societies, or is your character's purpose to create tension by being the person who wants something from the other village?**

It is important to remind the students that what the characters say and how they say it (their emotions and the tone, pitch and pace of the voice) will affect every aspect of this monologue. The monologues should be watched by the whole class and some of the monologues could be inserted into the scenes of the play.

Characters, mood and symbols

The following teaching strategies take place depending on where the playbuilders are situated in developing a strong dramatic story for their characters.

- Symbol: for example, each village could draw a symbol for their village which they could use as a flag or as a motif that they have on their clothes. They could create a chant or poem about or to their symbol and endow it with almost religious qualities if they want. Maybe the symbol is the object that the other village wants to have or to destroy.
- Mood: for example, mood could be explored by asking one village to create whispered arguments about an issue of importance that builds and builds in heightened secrecy, while the other village creates a very open celebration for an important tradition. Mood could also be explored by asking the class how stillness, sounds, music or lights might build the mood of the play.

Again, anything the playbuilders feel has significance from these improvisations could be refined and inserted as a scene into the play.

Phase three: structuring phase (about one week)

Refining dramatic meaning and audience engagement

Beginner playbuilders may have problems visualising their whole play in action and their scenes and characters may not be sharply focused. The following strategies could help them with this important aspect of playbuilding. Together the class writes or discusses:

- the final storyline;
- where the dramatic conflict is;
- how their characters have created this;
- scenes that are not working and need to be revised.

Another problem is scenes that lack character substance; this happens as students may have forgotten about the importance of acting and reacting to every moment or creating contrasting images, where perhaps one performer is still and the other moves quickly. To help solve these problems the teacher explains:

> The way a character performs an action reflects something about them, just as the way a character reacts to an action reflects something about them. So every moment of your play is about action and reaction and this is achieved vocally and physically and through maintaining a sharp focus to where the action is directed. Let's take a scene and workshop it so that you can all see what you need to try to achieve.

Another problem could be that the play is lacking subtext. If this is the case the teacher explains:

> Characters do not always openly reveal their concerns to each other. This is called subtext where there is another meaning going on underneath the dialogue and/or physical action. For example in your play, character X says: 'We must respect all differences', while opening their arms out in welcome, but the subtext is: 'I am afraid of these differences', and they would really like their arms to be tightly wrapped around themselves. The audience may know of this other implication, but in the main the other characters won't fully realise it. Where in your play does subtext occur and how can you heighten these moments?

All these types of problem can be overcome by refining individual scenes to solve the dramatic dilemma.

At this stage the play will most probably be 10 to 15 minutes long with scenes that don't necessarily link together. To help solve this linking problem and create dramatic meaning and audience engagement the teacher videos all the scenes, in sequence, and the students view them. As the playbuilders watch their play they discuss what linkings work and why, what needs to be linked in another way, or where it would be interesting to use a non-linear story structure by changing some of the scenes around.

Phase four: performative phase (about one week)

The elements of drama should be visible on the walls of the classroom and the teacher asks the students to read and discuss how they have incorporated these into their play. From this activity the playbuilders will refine their work through rehearsals. These rehearsals can be difficult for beginner playbuilders due to lack of experience, so the teacher breaks the rehearsal up into manageable moments by asking the group to perform it:

- first with the elements of drama in mind;
- secondly with props but no costumes;
- thirdly with costumes and props;
- lastly with costumes, props, lights and any production elements that are suitable.

This means that the teacher is slowly building up the rehearsal process by adding dramatic conventions that help the class to remain focused on their final task. The class should create a programme that reflects their learning about *differences* and they could perform their play to their peers or maybe to the local primary or infants' school.

Throughout the project the students have been regularly reflecting on their group story and what *differences* mean in the society they have created. Therefore when the individual students are completing the written component of the task they should be reminded to evaluate their story because of the different characters they created; this written assessment is handed in a week after the performance.

> *Handy hint . . .*
>
> *In the next unit of work it would be beneficial to continue reinforcing the importance of understanding the elements of drama.*

LOCATION-BASED PLAYBUILDING: USING LOCATION TO CREATE A STORY

Unit description

In this unit of work students explore how the location of a drama impacts on their playbuilding. Location-based playbuilding suits an episodic structure where situation, roles and characters respond to the dramatic tension of an episode in the chosen location. The teaching structure is for large groups to collaborate in the devising over a short time period. The reason for the different groupings and time structure to level 1 theme and character is that location-based playbuilding has different learning paths, in which students need to recognise and apply basic techniques and conventions before making and creating detailed location-based plays, as they do in levels 2 and 3.

How long?

The suggested timeline is 3 weeks based on 4 × 50-minute lessons a week.

Phase one: generative phase (about three lessons)

In the first lesson the teacher introduces the students to the importance of understanding stage geography in their location-based playbuilding. The teacher puts up an overhead or draws the stage geography on the whiteboard.

Understanding basic stage geography is helpful as it allows both the teacher and the students to refer accurately to the position of:

- the characters on the stage;
- set design objects on the stage.

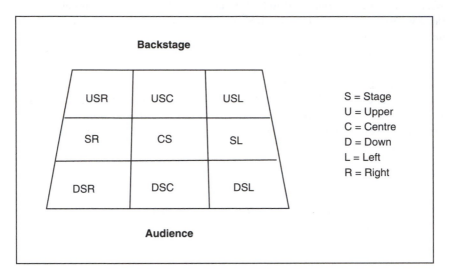

Figure 4.3 Stage geography (from the actor's point of view)

Beginner playbuilders will only use stage geography in a limited manner in this project, but it provides the building blocks to help them apply the techniques of systematically integrating actors and their location on a stage.

The students copy the diagram and abbreviations in their workbooks while the teacher explains that, using centre stage as a reference point, there are four other designated areas, stage right, stage left, upper stage and down stage. Upper stage is at the back, away from the audience, and down stage is closest to the audience. Stage right and left is always from the student actor's point of view looking out to the audience.

A student or students is asked to step into centre stage with their stage geography map. Members of the class ask them to be move stage right, left, and up and down the stage. The teacher then asks the student(s) to put their map(s) down and to move around the stage from memory telling the rest of the class their stage geography position.

An extension to this activity is to get two groups to work together each creating a scenario for the other. For example, a group could be asked to start stage left in a frozen position and run to upper stage right; from here they move in slow motion down stage left and then stroll back to centre stage, or they could be given written instructions to follow, using music as the rhythm for their exploration.

These activities are good fun and help the playbuilders to remember their stage geography. The next strategy is to teach the class how stage geography directly relates to a location.

The teacher explains:

> Stage geography also helps you understand how a set works in an imaginary location. We are going to build a simple set of a school location and explore this concept.

The teacher has created this set on the classroom floor and marked out the stage areas for easy reference. There are some tables and chairs on stage right, left and down stage right and left. This means the upper-stage areas, centre stage and down-stage centre are vacant. The teacher asks question about what type of school this is, what year group might inhabit this space and what time of day it is.

Some students are asked to take on the roles of pupils in this classroom and to sit in the appropriate places. Another student takes on the role of the teacher and uses either upper centre stage or down centre stage to create the teacher's prominent position in the classroom. When an imaginary bell rings, the teacher exits stage right or left and the pupils go around their desks to centre stage. They immediately endow centre stage as a playground area by playing handball, opening their sandwiches and lolling around.

The dramatic action is replayed and when the imaginary bell rings, two pupils take their chairs from the designated class areas into centre stage and endow this place as the Principal's office; one pupil becomes the Principal and the other is a pupil who is sitting in the office. The remaining pupils move upper-stage left and right and again make these areas into the school playground.

Discussion takes place on how the placement of objects on the set has allowed a number of different places in one location. The teacher reminds them that it will be important to use this technique in their forthcoming project as the plays they devise will depend partly on how their groups imagine a dynamic location.

Groupings

Random groups of 8 to 10.

> **Handy hint . . .**
> *Remind students about the importance of collaborating in playbuilding.*

Assessment of learning task

The class are handed out an assessment *of* learning task and read it through with their teacher.

Assessment *of* learning task

Each student is to collaborate in a group to create a 6–8-minute location-based play. The group can choose from any one of the following locations:

- an airport
- a cave
- a dungeon
- a forest
- a garden
- a kitchen
- a lift
- a school

- a streetscape
- a tower.

The criteria upon which the group will be assessed are as follows:

- The play should be episodic in structure: no more than four episodes and no less than two.
- The imagery of the set (i.e. the objects you use to create the set) should enhance the location.
- The location should be used as the focus of the episodes.
- Dramatic tension and conflict occurs within or because of the location.
- Your knowledge of stage geography must be evident in your workbooks through illustrations and notations of:
  - How you have used stage geography to understand where your role or character is on the stage at any given moment.
  - How your group has created a set to make an imaginary location on the stage floor.

In your workbook you are to write 150 words commenting on your individual and group processes and the importance of the group story in the designated location.

Each group would spend time discussing what starting point is of interest to them and why. They need to make an early decision; if there is indecision then a voting system can be organised so that the majority prevails.

Phases two and three: constructing and structuring phases (about one week)

Because of the nature of this type of playbuilding, groups will be constructing and structuring simultaneously. In these combined phases there are four teaching strategies which relate directly to the assessment criteria given to the students. After each strategy the teacher helps the groups to apply their leaning and at an appropriate time critiques their application.

It is important to start with episodic structure so that the whole class understands early on in the process how to go about this. The other teaching strategies are taught on a needs basis and the teacher decides whether it is better to work with the whole class or with individual groups.

Episodic structure

The teacher explains:

> Location-based playbuilding allows you to create episodes through incorporating various roles, characters and situations that all impact on your chosen location in different ways. Episodes have a similar structure to your favourite TV soaps but of

course yours will be much shorter; two or three minutes at most. Episodes are part of a serial story; each episode is distinct but contributes to the whole of the story about your location.

Episodes in this playbuilding project must be in the same location but they can be in different places and at different times. For example, using the starting point *A school* that you explored for stage geography, a group could have three different episodes:

- in a modern school room – twenty-first century;
- in a school room from the past – eighteenth century;
- in a school from the future – twenty-fifth century.

Each group must ask themselves these questions as they begin devising their play:

- What stories do you want to tell in your location and why?
- How many episodes do you want and why?
- What different time spans do you want and why?
- How will you link these episodes?

Imagery of the set

The groups should start creating their set while talking about the stories that might happen in each episode. They are given a worksheet to help them to understand how the imagery of their set should enhance their chosen location.

Worksheet
Your location needs to have a simple set so that the stage is not cluttered and so you can work actively in the space. Use this worksheet to walk around your developing set asking yourselves the following questions:

- What objects have you used to create the image of your location?
- Why has your group created the location in this way?
- How could you do it better?
- Will objects be moved from one episode to another and how will you do this?
- Does anything really have to be moved?

When each group has actively used this worksheet they should ask the teacher or their peers to look critically at what they are trying to achieve on their set.

Location and episodes

In this next teaching strategy the class becomes aware of how location can be used as a focus for the individual episodes they are developing. Again using the starting point of a *school* location the class are asked to recreate the set of the imaginary classroom. They are given the following scenario and a couple of students are asked to improvise it:

> Scenario
> A girl is studying at stage right. A boy enters stage right, crosses to stage left and sits at a desk and picks up a book. Looks are occasionally exchanged between the two pupils. Two teachers enter upper centre stage and move to centre stage as if they are in their staff room; they are discussing this girl and boy. The boy and girl freeze for a moment, creating a tableau. What will happen next?

The classes discuss how the drama has occurred simultaneously in two locations and how it enhances the storyline of this episode. The teacher explains that in this improvisation they have explored *broken* moments: first, the moment with the girl and boy that took place in the classroom; second, the moment in the staff room with teachers. These moments were *broken* in time by the use of the set to create different places in the same location, in the same timeframe. Through discussion and improvisations the individual groups apply this dramatic structure to moments in their developing stories and episodes.

Tension and conflict because of location

It is important for students to recognise that tension and conflict occur within and because of a location. The teacher asks the class to again recreate the set of the imaginary classroom.

A number of students become pupils who sit and stand upper-stage left; these pupils think it would be fun to taunt a studious pupil; they taunt non-verbally through bodily movement and rhythms which creates tension in the classroom. They must remain upper-stage left but react to every moment of the improvisation. Another student becomes the studious pupil; they are told that it is after school and they are studying in the classroom for an exam. They are sitting behind a school desk, stage right, with a textbook.

All students are in role as pupils and they respond to the side coaching of the teacher. The teacher asks all the pupils to do about 10 star jumps to get their bodies energised and then says:

> Pupils in the upper-stage left area are to begin non-verbally taunting the lone pupil sitting stage right; just for a few seconds. You are then to slowly add whispered sounds; these sounds must not get very loud but must become more threatening.
> Lone pupil you look up and react as if these pupils are about to chase you.
> Lone pupil run to the chair stage right, jump up on it and look around. Jump down running as fast as you can to down-stage left and crouch down behind the desks. Look out slowly and survey the location. Walk slowly and tentatively to centre stage and do a 360 degree turn looking out for trouble. You see them coming. Run down centre stage, a wall is in front of you; run into it with your arms spread out; freeze. Pupils upper-stage left run as fast as you can to down centre stage, increasing the volume of your whispered sounds and freeze two paces from the lone pupil.

The teacher discusses how the tension and conflict occurred within and because of the location. For example, the relationship between the characters changed and grew in tension because of where they were, or where they moved to on the set. There was a creation of surprise or shock at the end as the characters were almost in the audience's space, but an imaginary wall stopped them at the moment of conflict. The audience also did not know whether the lone pupil would get away or whether she or he would be caught and verbally taunted and physically hurt. Therefore the tension and conflict were enhanced by how the actors used the set to map out the story of the lone pupil trying to get away from the gang.

Each group is asked to reflect on their learning and to take a moment from one of their episodes and to map out the tension and conflict that happens in their location, taking into account how this can be enhanced by using their set and stage geography. At the end of the lesson each group demonstrates how they have tried to achieve this. This could be an assessment *for* learning activity so that the teacher knows if the groups understand the importance of using the location, set and stage geography to help them to devise their episodes.

Phase four: performative phase (about one week)

This last phase should start by helping each group to link their episodes. Students could:

- personify the location as a narrator, for example, they could record the *location's voice* on a CD which they play between one episode and the next;
- use the set to link their episodes; they could change an object's position on the set to create another mood and time;
- deliberately make transitions from one episode to another using centre stage. Centre stage is the most powerful focus area of a stage.

The class will also need to form the talking circle to discuss the assessment criteria and what they are achieving and what difficulties they are having. The teacher may need to work with each group individually to help solve and manage problems. Groups may need to:

- use an object from their set in a new way to create tension and/or conflict;
- explore their entrances and exits in relationship to the episodes;
- run through each episode with no objects or just one or two objects to create the location and discuss the advantages and disadvantages of doing this;
- map out their stage geography in their workbooks to help them solve problems of dramatic meaning.

As this project is only three weeks in duration the final performance may not be as polished as other projects, and the students should elect whether they would like to perform it to each other or if they would like an external audience. The class has continually reflected upon what they have learnt throughout the process, and each individual student needs to record a final reflection in their workbooks as well as to evaluate how they might use this learning in their next playbuilding project. The workbooks are handed in when practical.

Chapter 5

Level 2: intermediate playbuilders

Teaching considerations for intermediate playbuilders

At this level students have gained a solid depth and breadth of playbuilding skills, knowledge and understanding. As these students will have some experience in playbuilding the teacher will develop and extend their learning. This level of playbuilding involves students taking more responsibility for their own learning and gaining more confidence to think and act laterally. Collaboration in intermediate playbuilding continues to be very important and the class must understand that it plays a pivotal role in their creating. Groups of varying sizes and abilities should be explored in intermediate playbuilding. Those occasions where the class works as a whole group should now involve further challenges to extend the students, such as adding more constraints to the context being explored or through experimenting with different aspects of form and style.

In level 2 playbuilding, theme, character and location group-devised plays build upon level 1 as the teaching strategies reduce the level of dependence of the playbuilders on the teacher. Of course, when the playbuilders don't understand or make mistakes in their learning the teacher raises their teaching support to ensure progress, but it is important for the teacher to let control of the playbuilding be slowly transferred to the learner. The teaching strategies for intermediate playbuilders extend the students' skills, knowledge and understanding of the different ways to playbuild and present substantial learning challenges for the students.

Learner profile

Students who undertake level 2 playbuilding would have consistently engaged in drama education learning for 12 to 18 months and would have undertaken at least three to four playbuilding projects. By this stage these students will be ready to broaden and deepen their skills, knowledge and understanding of playbuilding processes. They will approach making, performing and reflecting with more dramatic curiosity and personal enjoyment as their playbuilding competency grows.

THEME-BASED PLAYBUILDING: EXPLORING THEME AND TEXT

Unit description

In this unit of work students experiment further with non-linear dramatic structures and characterisation to create a drama based on the theme of birthdays. They also engage in creative research that is then utilised within the playbuilding process. Students create a whole-class play that involves students working as a large group but the core of their work is done in smaller groups and structured to form the whole play. This unit is designed to challenge and extend students' skills by providing a more constrained context and narrative for playbuilding. The aim is to encourage students to deepen their character work, create more complex drama and experiment further with the elements of drama. The unit uses a piece of bare text as the pretext for the playbuilding process as well as other pieces of text to trigger ideas for characterisation and action. Students are encouraged to explore a range of fictional possibilities and link these narrative threads into a play about a single character. The unit focuses heavily on students working with the dramatic elements of role, focus, time and place to convey their drama. Techniques and conventions used aim to teach students about the elasticity of the art form as they work it into a shape that is both coherent and engaging. Students begin to consider the ways in which their work might resonate with different audiences.

How long?

This unit would normally take 5 weeks, with roughly 4 × 50-minute periods per week. Different aspects of the unit could easily be extended and more time could be devoted to particular tasks such as delving and experimenting with their research findings or developing each of their scenes further. If it is possible, more time devoted to these tasks would create an even richer final work.

Phase one: generative phase (about one week)

It is important to give the process a strong start by introducing the thematic content but also creating a strong collaborative and inquiring class environment. Students should be encouraged to experiment, ask questions and consider alternative ways of shaping their ideas and presenting them. Establishing and maintaining a healthy classroom climate for sharing and listening to ideas is critical to fostering good playbuilding practice.

Class discussion

Start the unit with a class discussion of the theme *Make a Wish*. Students could discuss:

- What kinds of things do people wish for? Why?
- Why do people make wishes on birthdays?
- What are the other times or occasions in people's lives where they might *make a wish* or engage in rituals that capture or communicate their wishes?

- Do different cultures have different ways of making wishes or making offerings? What practices and beliefs do we know about already?
- Would our wishes change with age? How would a wish of a 6-year-old differ to that of a 60-year-old?
- Does our context affect our wishes, for instance where we live or our level of wealth?
- Does gender affect the wishes we make? How?
- Do people often get their wishes? Why/why not? When?
- What happens if our wishes are not realistic or achievable? What could happen then?

Connecting with the themes

Ask students in pairs or small groups to share their own stories of memorable birthdays. These could be their own or someone else in their family or community. They then create a tableau, that captures the moment as it happened. Some of these are presented and discussed in relation to the theme. Students might consider what kinds of memories people have of birthdays and why these moments become lasting memories. They might also consider the other characters present in these scenes and how they might remember the occasion.

Groupings

The whole class works as an ensemble but the core of their work is done in smaller groups and structured to form the whole play

Assessment of learning task

This task is given to the students and discussed at the outset of the project, so that it clarifies for them the parameters of the project and the areas to be assessed. The teacher will need to consider when and how assessment evidence is to be recorded throughout the project. Learning experiences which may be good opportunities for teachers to assess students in the making phase of the work are marked with an asterisk ★ in the plan that follows.

Assessment *of* learning task

The class will create a play that explores the themes of wishes and birthdays. The play will show one character's journey through life. There will be scenes involving the whole class and also small groups within the play. The class will create the play together and agree on its content, structure and meaning. In small groups you will develop and shape your ideas into scenes which will contribute to the play as a whole. The play will use an episodic structure and will show critical moments and characters who contribute to this person's life. At points in the playbuilding process you will engage in research that helps to generate ideas and enhance the drama. You will be expected to discuss the work as it develops and evaluate both your own and others' drama work. You will also be expected to listen to the feedback of others and take it on board as you create your own scenes. The play will be performed for at least two audiences – one audience of similar-aged students and one audience of adults. Your teacher will assess your drama skills and understandings throughout the project.

Making the drama
- Contribute interesting ideas that advance the development of the work.
- Demonstrate a sound understanding of role, time and place as elements of drama.
- Develop, portray and sustain characters in improvisations.
- Make strong and effective choices about character, action and narrative to engage the audience.
- Engage in useful research that enhances the playbuilding process.
- Weave ideas from the research into the scene work to strengthen the drama.
- Utilise the feedback to enhance and strengthen your own work.

Performing the drama
- Sustain and convey character in performance in an engaging way.
- Employ the elements of drama effectively in performance.
- Support the stage action and other players effectively.

Reflecting on the drama
- Evaluate the effectiveness of your own drama work.
- Evaluate the effectiveness of others' work.
- Reflect on the dramatic impact of the drama and the way it engages.

All the world's a stage

This activity begins with a discussion about performance and how performance is part of our everyday lives. Students could consider the contexts and situations where we might play a part or role (e.g. school, work, at a family gathering, online) and why we play roles in everyday life. The class discusses the opening line from Jacques' speech in Shakespeare's *As You Like It* ('All the world's a stage, and all the men and women merely players'). What does this mean? Is it true? Are we players? How?

The teacher then leads a discussion about how the dramatic art form works. Some points to be considered could be:

- How theatre reworks the performances of everyday life and re-presents them to an audience through careful selection of character, story, action and dramatic elements.
- The stage becomes a dynamically charged space where worlds are created and constructed and everyday stories and experiences are heightened and re-imagined for an audience. Skilled dramatists and devised theatre companies know how to carefully exploit the language of the stage and its elements to evoke particular imagery or responses from their audiences.
- Drama activates what playwright Brian Friel calls the *collective mind* of the audience. Teachers may wish to give out this quote and discuss it at length with the class:

> theatre can be experienced only in community with other people . . . the dramatist functions through the group, not a personal conversation but a public address . . . Of course his concern is to communicate with every individual in that

audience, but he can only do that through the collective mind. If he cannot get the attention of that collective mind, hold it, persuade it, mesmerise it, manipulate it, he has lost everything. And this imposes strange restrictions on him because the collective mind is a peculiar mind.

(Friel 1999, p.18)

From this quote the class might discuss:

- the actor–audience relationship;
- the notion of the audience as active meaning makers in the performance;
- the many ways in which audiences could be *engaged*;
- what performance issues might affect that engagement.

The class then reads the whole of Jacques' speech and discusses its ideas.

All the World's a Stage

All the world's a stage,
And all the men and women merely players;
They have their exits and their entrances;
And one man in his time plays many parts,
His acts being seven ages. At first the infant,
Mewling and puking in the nurse's arms;
Then the whining school-boy, with his satchel
And shining morning face, creeping like snail
Unwillingly to school. And then the lover,
Sighing like furnace, with a woeful ballad
Made to his mistress' eyebrow. Then a soldier,
Full of strange oaths, and bearded like the pard,
Jealous in honour, sudden and quick in quarrel,
Seeking the bubble reputation
Even in the cannon's mouth. And then the justice,
In fair round belly with good capon lin'd,
With eyes severe and beard of formal cut,
Full of wise saws and modern instances;
And so he plays his part. The sixth age shift
Into the lean and slipper'd pantaloon,
With spectacles on nose and pouch on side;
His youthful hose, well sav'd, a world too wide
For his shrunk shank; and his big manly voice,
Turning again toward childish treble, pipes
And whistles in his sound. Last scene of all,
That ends this strange eventful history,
Is second childishness and mere oblivion;
Sans teeth, sans eyes, sans taste, sans everything.
        Jacques (Act II, Scene VII, lines 139–166)

Then, in seven small groups students create each of the different ages in the life of man. They are to convey a non-verbal scene that shows the *man*, the dramatic context of the age (with other characters). If there is space, designate each group a part of the space to work in, in order. When they show and share their work, they are to run each scene back to back, rolling the scenes out one by one, in a montage effect (as each one ends, the other begins). Music could be played to enhance this presentation.

After these scenes are shown, the class can discuss the way they were communicated and the ideas they generated about human experience. Ask the students to consider how different-aged audiences might react to these different scenes and why. Some of these ideas can be revisited later in the playbuilding process if necessary. In their workbooks students can reflect upon the lesson content and workshop scenes. They can write about which ones stood out and why. Encourage students to use drama terminology and the elements of drama to discuss their peers' work.

Phase two: constructing phase (about two weeks)

This unit focuses on creating a play that portrays a single character's journey through time, with the theme of *the birthday wish* as the recurring theme to show the changes of time, character and context. As a group, students will gradually build a coherent drama that features different episodes in time and captures different voices and perspectives in relation to this character. It is important to give time to class and group discussion each lesson, regularly checking in and recording each new development in the dramatic structure and narrative.

Bare text as pretext for playbuilding

A bare script has no identifiable characters, emotions, situation, time or location. The bare scripts are useful as students can have the freedom to explore their own ideas but with learning restrictions. Give students the following short piece of bare text and discuss who they could be, where, when and what ideas the dialogue generates for them:

[Five characters on stage]

A:	What a special day.
B:	Just for you!
C:	Everyone is here now.
D:	Are you happy, love?
A:	You should be.
B:	So lucky . . . so fortunate.
C:	Such a beautiful cake.
D:	Remember this day always, alright?
B:	Okay . . . are you ready?
A:	Take a deep breath . . . and . . .
ALL:	Make a wish!

In groups of five, students discuss their own interpretation of the dialogue, adding character and context to the piece. Students must make a strong attempt to convey the age of the character having the birthday. Students prepare the scene as a whole piece at first.

After 5–10 minutes of working, students are asked to select one line and a group freeze that they feel best sums up their scene. These are presented and *read* by the class. What is being conveyed in each scene? What is being foregrounded or emphasised by each group? What do we think is happening in each scene? How do we know? How has the group focused the scene? What is the effect on the audience? The teacher can link the discussion back to activities last lesson where the class discussed the notion of the audience being active meaning makers, making their own meanings from the work.

The groups then return to work on the scene as a whole, this time adding and incorporating the input from their peers. They modify the scene to extend it and make their ideas clearer or sharper. Each group presents their scenes in full and these are discussed by the class. What new ideas have emerged, now we see the whole scene? What images and responses emerge for the audience now? What do they notice about the characters in each scene?

Focusing the drama*

The teacher then explains that one of these scenes will become the nucleus of the class play. The challenge for the class will be now to create a whole work around one of these main characters. To do this some groups will need to modify their scenes to accommodate the character shift. The teacher helps the class to decide on one character whose life story might be the most interesting to develop. This may not necessarily be the most exciting or overly dramatic character. Often plays show the extraordinary sides to ordinary lives or situations. Students discuss the possibilities in focusing on each potential main character. In their groups students now modify and rework their previous scenes to convey the same character and their different birthdays over time. Remind students of the earlier activity, where they depicted the seven ages of man, they may wish to draw on some earlier ideas. Students may need some help to reach a consensus as to how old the character should be in each scene and how they might adapt their previous scenes. These are shown and discussed at length. What needs to be developed in each scene to make a more coherent life story for this character? What needs to be agreed and shown consistently in each group's scene? What new layers to this character are emerging now?

These birthday scenes must now show the character and their context at different times in his or her life. Replay the reworked scenes in chronological order of time, from the earliest of birthdays to the last. On the board make a timeline of the character's life, showing when each birthday occurs and what the focus of each scene is. These birthday scenes will provide the thematic link or thematic through line for the play as a whole. The class may change them in the final play, so the work doesn't become too repetitive. The class discusses the use of recurring motifs in plays and how they work to give emphasis to ideas or episodes in the action.

Focusing on the main character

Each group now discusses the main character that is emerging in the work and completes a role on the wall activity (see Needlands and Goode 1990 for a full explanation of this strategy). On big sheets of card or paper they draw a figure and inside it write words to describe their interpretation of the main character (in general). Outside the figure they are to note down what's at stake for this character at this point in their lives or what issues are critical to this character at this point. These are shared and discussed. If possible these can be placed around the space for future reference.

In the same small groups students now create a scene that shows another moment in the character's life. It can be:

- a memorable moment;
- an ordinary moment/slice of life moment;
- a moment or experience that influenced who they are as an adult.

In their scene students are to focus on showing the main character's perspective of the event or moment. These are shared with the class and discussed in terms of the new details that are emerging about the character and their story. On the board or in students' workbooks, record a short description of the moment and the key characters present in each scene.

> *Research task 1*
> At home or school students are to interview two or more people who share a memory of the same event; they can be family members or members of the same year group. These people are interviewed and asked about what they remember about that event. Students should try to get basic facts as well as how they reacted to the event. Compare the different versions of the same story. What things do they notice about how we remember events? Are our memories accurate? What factors influence our memories?

Same scene, different perspective*

In their groups, students discuss their research findings. They now use some of their findings to assist them in reworking the last scene, this time from a different character's point of view. These are presented to the class and discussed in terms of the new insights this alternative version presents. The class can then discuss how dramatists might juxtapose contrasting scenes or views in a play to show how complex scenes and relationships can be, or to create a sense of intrigue or ambiguity.

Duologue exploring character relationships

An assessment *for* learning activity could be that in pairs students construct a short rehearsed improvisation that shows a scene between the main character and one other character, sometime in the past. It should be a character who has emerged already in the playbuilding. It can be a moment in the immediate past or further in time. This is a moment that only these two characters know and share.

These duologues are presented to the class. For each duologue allocate another pair who will give feedback about the scene in terms of:

- new insights about character and relationship;
- how the scene adds to the narrative about the main character and his or her life;
- the effectiveness of the scene.

- the use of the elements of drama;
- what could be enhanced or extended to make the scene stronger.

Students can record key points made in their workbooks, so they can refer to them later as they refine and rehearse their scenes.

Phase three: structuring phase (about one week)

For this phase of the work it is important for the teacher to lead the decision-making process as students recall the work so far and negotiate a workable effective dramatic structure. Not all the scenes and ideas generated to date will be able to be used in the final play.

The first step is to create a map of the materials they have generated. This can be done on the board or online or on paper. It is important for the class to discuss once again the theme and what they would like to communicate about it to their audience. The teacher needs to lead a class discussion about dramatic structure and the impact of variety and non-linear structure on the audience. Because the students have generated much of the play's content already, the work should have its own logic and coherence by this stage. With the teacher's guidance, the class decides on the basic dramatic structure of the play. They use the bare text episodes as the recurring motif, but in selecting the key scenes, they should alternate different timeframes and perspectives for dramatic effect.

The class then discusses what needs to be modified or changed to fit the new structure of the work. In particular the bare text scenes will need work as they will act as linking scenes. Possible strategies for the students to consider could be:

- playing the scene in full in a realistic way;
- freezing a moment from the scene with a single line, possibly a different one each time;
- using slow motion or robotic movement alongside realistic dialogue;
- using the space creatively to focus the audience's attention in the scene.

Refining and rehearsing the new structure

It is important for students to now get a sense of how the dramatic structure feels in the space. Methodically they work through each scene, refining and amending at first, then rehearsing each scene more fully. It is important for the class to discuss the problems they face at this point as they refine the work and work together to resolve the issues and strengthen each scene for an effective performance.

> *Research task 2 – conveying time and place through the scene linkages*
> Each student selects one research focus and finds one or two short examples that could be used to convey the time and place of one of the scenes they have devised. They can choose to find:
>
> - music from the period;
> - visual imagery – photographs from the period;

- sound effects – cars, trams, trains, footsteps;
- text – e.g. newspaper headlines or reports.

These are shared and the class discusses which of these could be used to link the scenes and how. Students experiment with how these research findings might be incorporated into the scenes or used to link different scenes.

After Friel: using monologues and movement to open and close the play*

The class now works together to create two key monologues from the main character's point of view that will be used at the beginning and at the end of the play. The teacher shows the class the opening and closing scenes from Brian Friel's play *Dancing at Lughnasa* (1990). They discuss the techniques used and how juxtaposing monologue and tableau as well as monologue and movement can create visual and narrative impact in the space. The discussion could also address the issue of dramatic closure and the way works might leave a final impact or message with their audience.

Divide the class in half: one group works on the opening monologue and the other on the closing. Working in small groups students create a short monologue and experiment with Friel's techniques. These are shown and discussed. The class then selects what is strongest or most impactful (some synthesis of ideas and words may need to be done at this point). These become the opening and closing scenes of the play.

Phase four: performative phase (about one week)

Once the play has been structured, the students can now begin to rehearse the play in full. The class will need to decide on some basic production elements such as the use of symbolic costume, props and lighting. This play focuses on the story and the ensemble sharing, conveying it collectively, so these elements could be used sparingly to enable different actors to step into key roles.

It is important to perform the play at least twice for different-aged audiences: peers but also an older audience from their community (perhaps an audience of senior citizens could be invited). This play has focused on human experience and the impact of time and place on one person's life, so the age and positioning of the audience would be interesting for the students to consider and analyse. After they perform their work, students can discuss the play with their audiences or construct a quick audience survey or response sheet to get a sense of the way the work affected their different audiences. The feedback from the audiences would provide strong focal points for reflection. They could consider the way their play engaged their audience and the nuances of the actor–audience relationship they were able to create. Another useful point for reflection would be Friel's notion of the collective mind of the audience and its peculiarity. The class can discuss or write about their reflections on the quote. Students should also reflect upon their learning experience as a whole. What new understandings has this project given them about playbuilding and the art form? What do they need to continue to work on in terms of their playbuilding skills (as a class and individually)? This could be the focus of a final piece of reflective writing, based on the project.

CHARACTER-BASED PLAYBUILDING: INVENTING PHYSICAL CHARACTERS

Unit description

In this unit of work, playbuilders are given the opportunity to create characters from their external appearance to their internal thoughts and feelings. This character-based playbuilding requires students to explore their character's physicality and then to find ways to internalise this physicality so that they develop a fully rounded character. They will explore the genre of a suspense thriller to create their play.

How long?

Suggested timeline is 5 weeks based on 4 × 50-minute lessons per week.

Phase one: generative phase (about one week)

This unit of work is based on the student's physicality so it is very important to regularly run warm-ups that allow students to recognise and explore the importance of their body. In the first couple of lessons the teacher introduces tag games and movement exercises that energise the students' bodies and hence their minds. From these activities the class are introduced to the importance of using their entire body to create characters.

The class are asked to walk around the room and follow the side-coaching of the teacher; they stop after each exploration to discuss what type of character is emerging and why:

- Brush your hair and admire your bodies in an imaginary mirror.
- Walk with large strides and start bounding across the room.
- Wave delicately at every passer-by and tiptoe to a chair to sit down.
- Saunter across the room and sit down with a swagger.
- Pull a face then add the walk that goes with it.

Other physical actions that could be explored are characters that move off-balance, or move far too quickly, or move diagonally or in circles across the space, or ones who do not want to move at all. Before or after these types of improvisations the teacher discusses the importance of knowing intimately the external physical demands of a character, as this aspect of character development helps them to sustain a fully realised character, with an emotional internal life, in their playbuilding project.

Groupings

Mixed-ability groups with 5 or 6 in a group. *Inventions* is going to be the starting point for the playbuilding project and in the next improvisation students begin exploring the possibilities of this topic. The groups that are now formed should be the ones used in the actual playbuilding project.

The teacher explains:

Inventions are created by people who see a need or a problem in society and who attempt to find a solution to it. In this improvisation you will be creating images of inventions from the past and you can do this literally or in an abstract manner. In your improvisation try to demonstrate the invention's function and purpose, and a past or present society's reaction to it. This improvisation is based on exaggerated physicality and you can use dialogue if appropriate.

Each group will be given 15 minutes to create their invention and then we will watch them all.

Group 1: Dental surgery (seventh millennium BC)
Group 2: Soap (third millennium BC)
Group 3: Perfume (second millennium BC)
Group 4: Glassblowing (one millennium BC)
Group 5: Gunpowder (one millennium CE).

> **Handy hint . . .**
> For some classes it might be more appropriate to give them more challenging inventions from the twenty-first century.

After they have performed these improvisations they discuss:

- the way that different groups demonstrated the purpose and function of the invention;
- how groups used their physicality to create the scene;
- what these scenes might say to an audience.

Phase two: constructing phase (about one week)

Assessment of learning task

This phase begins with the class, in their groups, reading through the assessment of learning task and the teacher clarifying points of misunderstanding.

> **Assessment of learning task**
>
> *Starting point: The Inventors*
> Each group is to collaborate to create a 15-minute play around the given starting point.
>
> The play's focus must be on a real or imagined invention from any time period as well as the purpose and function of the invention.
>
> The performance style of the play will be the suspense thriller genre. Your suspense thriller should have a single dramatic goal that drives the tension of the drama forward. Your play should therefore contain cliff-hanging tension which takes your audience on a suspenseful journey.
>
> Each student will develop one character, but if a group wishes to explore abstract ideas, such as all or some becoming the invention, they can do so in conjunction

with their character. The group must decide which character is the protagonist and which the antagonist and what the other characters' relationships are to one another.

Process and performance assessment criteria
Each student will be assessed on their ability to:

- work collaboratively with others in the playbuilding task;
- use research material as a tool in the playbuilding process;
- contribute to the storyline of their play;
- contribute to the creation of the suspense thriller genre;
- create a character from external body to internal motivations;
- demonstrate a character's strengths and weaknesses;
- demonstrate a character's motivation;
- use voice and dialogue to enhance their character;
- develop and sustain their character in relationship to other characters;
- adjust to unforeseen circumstances in the process and final performances;
- display a high level of competence in performance;
- work independently of the teacher.

Workbook
When you hand in your workbook a week after the performance it must be up to date and be a record and reflection on your processes and final performance.
   The workbook will be assessed on each student's individual ability to discuss:

- how your group explored performance skills appropriate to the playbuilding;
- how your group developed and sustained a suspense thriller structure;
- how your group incorporated pertinent research;
- how your group managed and solved problems;
- how you individually developed and sustained your character's physical and emotional life;
- what you have learnt about the diverse approaches of your group to making the play;
- how you and your group responded to the audience's reaction to your play.

The teacher asks each group to answer these questions before improvising their initial ideas; the answers provide the groups with a framework to build improvisations upon:

- What is an invention?
- Why do people invent?
- Do people invent just for the benefit of society?
- What categories of inventions are there?
- What happens to an invention?
- Why are some inventions valued more than others?
- What would our world be without inventions?

The teacher has arranged a session in the library where the groups research inventions. They are also encouraged to ask the science, design and technology teachers about their views on different categories of inventions. After this initial research the whole class comes together for one lesson to learn how to create a play of the suspense thriller genre. The class brainstorms the characteristics of this genre (which they will probably know through film, television and novels) and the teacher provides the expert knowledge to help them clarify their thoughts.

> The suspense thriller genre is a fast-paced play where the protagonist is generally in danger, so a sense of being hunted or exposed to danger is an important aspect of your play. It can be a psychological play where characters prey on each other's mind to get what they want or it can be classified as a hunt where characters are more exposed to danger on a physical level; or it can be a combination of both. When collaboratively creating the play your group should include some of the following dramatic techniques which can be applied or adapted to your group's particular context. For example:
>
> - intense excitement and a high level of anticipation and uncertainty within the story;
> - a protagonist (leading character or characters) and an antagonist (a leading enemy or enemies);
> - characters that know they are exposed to danger on a mental and physical level;
> - characters that don't know they are exposed to danger on a mental and physical level;
> - characters with strong motives who possess strong emotional and physical traits;
> - characters that are desperate and hopeless;
> - a first-person narrative character who can involve the audience directly as their confidant;
> - the backstory (the history behind the story), for example the motivations to get the invention patented or even stolen;
> - an unusual location which could open up possibilities for different types of characters and their adventure;
> - an unexpected denouement; the final unravelling of the plot;
> - a nerve-wracking adventure that takes your audience on an exciting journey.

This information could be handed out as a worksheet.

In this playbuilding it is very important for the groups to make decisions early on about the story and plotline of their play. The following are a number of teaching strategies to help the groups reach these decisions. They should:

- Name their play.
- Write up the storyline in chronological time order.
- Write a focus statement about their play and then write down:

  ○ Event 1
  ○ Event 2

- ○   Event 3
- ○   Climax
- ○   Denouement.

- Ask one group member to give a verbal summary of the play while the other members of the group listen. The student talking can be interrupted only if another student does not have the same vision. This student then takes over the process; this is repeated until someone tells the summary without interruption. When this happens it is a very good idea for all the group members to write down the agreed summary in their workbooks.

After these types of activities the talking circle is formed and each group shares their developing story with the class. For example, one group might be creating a suspense thriller about the invention of a pill that keeps people forever youthful and its focus is on greed and envy or another group may have created a story around the invention of a new religion and its focus is on distrust, or another group may be exploring how people get rich through inventions and its focus is on blackmail. These shared conversations are used as an assessment *for* learning tool by the teacher who gathers information about how each group is making their suspense thriller and if they need help in creating a more robust metaphoric story with stronger characters.

Phase three: structuring phase (about two weeks)

The following drama techniques can be taught to individual groups at different times mutually agreed upon. This means that the group sets their own learning goals. These techniques are explored through discussion and improvisation, and recorded and reflected in the workbook.

Character development

With the teacher the groups explore how to develop and sustain their characters. The following teaching strategies concentrate on physical expression that gives rise to the internal identification of a character. It is important for the playbuilders to understand that this acting is precise, a little exaggerated, and the characters are, in general, not stereotypical, so the students have to continually find this balance.

Character motivation

Every student writes out what their character's motivation is in the play and shares this with the rest of their group. Sometimes groups are surprised by what they hear and the motivation of characters has to be revised, or this activity may give rise to deeper discussions about the multifaceted nature of a character's motivation that helps create dramatic meaning in their scenes.

Using the body to express attitude

The teacher asks the students, in character, to stand in front of a mirror and to physically emphasise the movement of their eyes to express an attitude to the invention. They may wish to express disbelief, joy, surprise, distain, fear, greed and they can add sound if they wish. The students, in character, extend this activity by adding individual body parts to strengthen this physical attitude; they begin with their faces, then arms, legs, torso and whole body. They discuss how isolating different body parts can help them to develop precisely their character's attitude to the invention and to each other.

Exploring animals' characteristics to develop character

Each group discusses how the characteristics of animals can actively relate to the developing personalities of their characters. The teacher asks the different groups to watch a relevant film or television programme for homework and to give feedback to their peers, discussing which professional actors they think have developed their characters from observing animals and why.

The groups should also discuss the characteristics of different animals, which will help them to develop their character's physicality as well as to explore ways to bring this external physicality inside themselves so that their character has an internal life. For example, the teacher poses the following type of questions:

- What are the characteristics of a cockerel, a mule, a cat, a dove?
  - Cockerels crow every morning and strut around; they are the lords of their domain.
  - Cats slowly stalk their prey and leisurely clean themselves; they can be faithful or unfaithful companions depending on their mood.
  - Mules plod slowly and thoughtfully whilst working; they are stubborn and self-willed.
  - Doves coo melodically and swoop and glide through the air, but they always return to the dove cote.

- How does an animal's physicality indicate their temperament?
- Animals can be representative of certain types of people: why?
- Why use an animal to help develop a character's physicality? What does this add to the external and internal life of a character?
- Where can you observe animals?
- How could you apply this observation to your characterisation and a character's motives in the play?

The teacher asks the groups to work collaboratively to decide what type of animal or animals suits each of the characters they are developing. The group improvises these animal characteristics and applies these explorations to their developing characters' physicality and personalities.

> *Handy hint . . .*
> *An excursion to the zoo to observe animal behaviour and movements is a great extension to this teaching strategy.*

Using objects

Each student is asked to bring an object of importance to their character into this improvisation. The object can be the invention, part of the invention, or perhaps a personal prop. The teacher explains that objects from the drama they are creating can be used physically to make a dramatic point.

In pairs, with one character using their object, they:

- point it threateningly at their partner and glare;
- place it near their heart and smile;
- let it rest on their hands in contemplation and gaze out;
- move it quickly as if fanning their partner's face;
- drop it suddenly and frown;
- hide it on their person and smirk.

The pairs repeat this activity with the other student taking a turn, and add dialogue this time around. Again the groups discuss how they can use objects in the scenes of their play to create suspense and how the dialogue created tension through its volume, pace, pitch, tone and stresses on certain words or sounds.

Status

The groups need to think how they will manipulate and use each character's status in a perceptive and creative way in the scenes of their plays. The status of a character in a suspense thriller is determined by factors such as a character's knowledge, skills, wisdom, wealth, power in relationship to the invention.

The teacher asks the students to create images of their characters' relationship to the invention at the *beginning, middle* and *end* of the play. This should demonstrate how a character's status changes during the suspense thriller play and this should be clear to the audience. If the groups are having some difficulties, the teacher reminds them that often a higher-status character will dominate the space by the way they stand, walk, sit, use their eyes, and talk and a lower-status character will achieve the opposite, but that all this should be achieved subtly.

The teacher poses questions that have to be physically and verbally solved by the group:

- How does a character's physicality affect the status of their characters?
- How does a character's status shift and change throughout the play?
- What are the social conditions and relationships created in the scenes of the play that cause a character's status to change?
- How does the invention affect each character's status?
- How does dialogue affect the status of their characters?

Developing dialogue

Each group discusses in detail the dialogue that is developing and how it moves the suspense thriller along. They should also discuss why their characters speak in a certain way and what particular idiosyncrasies they may have in their language patterns. For example, do some characters talk at each other, do others talk like a summer breeze, do others talk like a raging storm, do some stutter and are others verbose?

After all these activities, the groups should try to apply what they have learnt to their developing scenes and characters.

Worksheet to develop the play

The students are given a worksheet to help them develop their ideas further.

- Name your suspense thriller.
- Name the invention.
- What is your character's name and age?
- What does your character think about this invention? Why?
- Is your character in the protagonist's camp, the antagonist's camp, or somewhere in between?
- What motivates your character to behave as she or he does? Write down some of your dialogue that proves your point of view.
- Is your character based on an animal? If yes, what, why and how? If no, how have you physically developed your character?
- Describe your character's voice and how this relates to your character's physicality?
- Do you have an object that enhances your character's physical actions? How does it do this?
- What is your character's status throughout the play? Does it change? When and why?
- Write a paragraph about the play from your character's point of view.

Scenes and links

A suspense thriller needs to be linked seamlessly so that the fast pace does not drop and so that the dramatic action builds and builds. Groups can experiment with this by:

- never using a blackout except when they want to create a suspenseful atmosphere;
- using a first-person narrator to fast-track the danger;
- using the invention, in the links, to carry the tension forward;
- finishing each scene on the upbeat so that the audience knows something even more terrifying is going to happen next;
- planting clues at the end of each scene that can be solved in the next scene;
- allowing the audience to learn something new at the end of each scene that links to the next scene.

The teacher could give the students an example of what their suspense thriller play may look like. Each group should attempt to make up their own map.

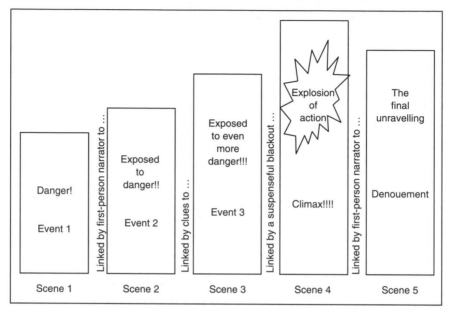

Figure 5.1 How a suspense thriller may evolve

Phase four: performative phase (about one week)

In this last phase one of the major problems will be to help the groups create the fast pace that is needed in a suspense thriller. The groups can try to achieve this fast pacing by:

- standing in a circle and creating a clapping rhythm for their play; if the rhythm falters they all need to say where they think they are in the play's structure and why some students have created a different rhythm;
- experimenting with running the play in double time on the stage floor;
- having numerous line runs where no pauses are allowed.

They should refine these types of activities until they have perfected the play's pacing. The plays should be simply costumed, with minimal sets, lighting and sound to complement the students' work. Each group should create their own suspense thriller programme.

These plays should be performed to a public audience where the students can have a night of suspense and thrillers; maybe they can invite the science classes or design and technology classes to be the audience and have a discussion about their inventions afterwards (both the inventiveness of their play and the invention they chose to dramatise). The playbuilders need to be reminded that after the performance they have to complete their workbooks as per the outline of the assessment *of* learning task. They will need to draw on their verbal and written reflections of their making and performing processes, which will enable them to judge the learning opportunities that this project has given them.

LOCATION-BASED PLAYBUILDING: DEVISING FOR DIFFERENT SPACES

Unit description

Level 2 location-based playbuilding gives students the opportunity to collaboratively create a play in a location outside their classroom. Students will devise a play that is to be performed outdoors, using simple visual street theatre techniques. This type of play-building may use some of the conventions, techniques and performance styles of street and event theatre and site-specific theatre but the concepts of playbuilding where all students are creating collaboratively and contributing equally are the focus of the work. This unit challenges intermediate playbuilders to collaborate in large groups using a range of techniques to create a visual spectacle and communicate their ideas to their audience, conveying their ideas in more presentational and exaggerated ways.

For the purposes of safety and convenience we have omitted the use of lanterns and fire, often used by Welfare State International (UK) as part of their community-based projects. Teachers will need to consider whether lantern making and processions are suitable for their context and performance event. There are substantial safety issues to consider when using lanterns in performance.

How long?

The suggested timeline is 8 weeks based on 4 × 50-minute lessons per week. Should the class decide to use more elaborate puppets and masks, there may be more time needed for construction and rehearsal.

Phase one: generative phase (about one week)

The first part of this unit introduces students to the form, some key considerations when using this form, and also some of the techniques they will need to utilise in their play-building. Students complete a practice task as a class so they become aware of the kinds of decisions they will need to make for their main assessment task. This scaffolds the students' playbuilding and sets the terrain for exploration.

Groupings

The main task for this unit involves the students working in large groups of 8–10 group members. Such a group size will be challenging in the early phases of devising but will be necessary as they perform. Students will need many hands to operate and manipulate the various production elements and effects they have created, particularly if they choose to devise a mobile or processional performance. These larger groups might make decision making and consensus harder at times. The teacher will need to keep the groups focused and on task at every step. These large groups will need to work effectively and quickly to develop the work and realise their intentions in performance.

Understanding this form of theatre

Students will need to understand that this form of theatre is recognisably different to text-based forms and theatre that is housed in a purpose-built building. Its focus, content and conventions are often far more accessible, participatory and popular. As a way of introducing the project the following topics could be the subject of teacher-led lessons, internet and book research or practical workshops.

Traditions

This form of theatre is closely linked to folk arts, events and festivals. There are many folk art traditions around the world and it is possible to find parallel theatre forms and techniques across decades and countries. There is a strong historical through line in popular theatre forms in the Western theatre tradition from the Greeks right through to medieval carnivals and parades, *commedia dell' arte* to more recent forms of agit-prop, political theatre, vaudeville, circus and cabaret. Many countries have forms of puppetry or masked theatre and other ritualised performance traditions that appeal to ordinary people and rely on archetypal characters and use local myths and stories. Such forms utilise comedy as well as elements of carnival and spectacle to communicate their stories and celebrate cultural events and places of significance.

Key tenets

- Based in communities and is about community concerns and events.
- Uses symbols or icons that are recognisable to the community.
- Theatre for the people by the people – principles of access and participation are essential.
- People's theatre that can be celebratory or subversive and/or political in its nature. Aims to be entertaining and engaging while also commenting on serious social or political issues. Can focus on issues such as anti-consumerism, anti-war or anti-globalisation issues.

Definitions

- *Street theatre* – theatre that is devised for and performed on the street, usually for an audience of passers-by. It often has political or social messages and has to be engaging and hold the audience's attention. This type of theatre often makes use of techniques that invite audience participation in the performance event. (See Sue Fox's chapter in Coult and Kershaw's *Engineers of the Imagination: The Welfare State Handbook*, 1999, pp.31–41 as a thorough discussion of some of the core issues to consider when creating a piece of street theatre.)
- *Site-specific theatre* – theatre which is made for a particular site rather than a theatrical building, usually an outdoor or public space. The site is a key influence in the devising process and is an intrinsic part of the performance event. Often the site dictates the content and conventions to be used. (John Fox's book *Eyes on Stalks* would be useful further reading on this type of theatre.)
- *Event theatre* – celebrates a particular event that has significance for a particular com-

munity, place or family. Often uses processional forms such a parades and processional theatre, where either the performance moves through the space or the audience is mobile, moving from stage to stage (like in medieval times or carnivals).

Core elements

- Uses and blends multiple art forms and processes for theatrical purposes, where visual arts, dance and music feature in the devising and performing of the work. This means that the devisers are also the makers of the objects, sets and music as well as dramatists and performers in the finished work.
- Uses spectacle and visual elements to create larger-than-life effects and scenarios.
- Recognisable themes, characters and stories to appeal to the audience.
- Uses improvised scenarios.
- Purpose to celebrate or entertain, sometimes to inform or protest.
- Uses a range of techniques simultaneously – puppetry, masks, banners, music, lanterns, poetry, storytelling, mime, direct address to the audience, often engaging the audience directly.
- Can use a specific site or landscape to create, design and be utilised in performance, moving theatre outside the theatre building.
- Has aspects of community celebration and ritualised elements, often drawing its symbols and ideas from within the community it serves.

Practitioners and examples

There are a number of innovative more contemporary companies that offer interesting examples of practice and viewpoints about their highly visual, alternative brand of popular, street or community theatre. To support the learning, teachers can extend the unit by inviting students to study popular theatre from around the world and the work of particular theatre practitioners working in highly visual forms such as Phillipe Genty (France) and companies such as Welfare State International (UK), the Bread and Puppet Theatre (UK), the San Francisco Mime Troupe (USA), and Odin Teatret (Denmark).

Important considerations

In small groups students now begin to consider some critical issues that impact the creation of a piece of street/outdoor theatre. Give each group one of the following considerations to focus on:

- purpose
- demands of the site
- event/occasion
- audience
- production issues
- safety issues and weather considerations.

For each consideration ask the students to brainstorm as a group:

- What are the critical issues a street theatre company may face?
- What are the possible strategies they might employ to address these issues?

These should be shared and discussed at length, possibly referring back to any earlier examples or research done, to look for ways existing companies addressed these issues. These notes could then be collated, copied and placed in students' workbooks for reference when they are further on in their own playbuilding process.

Practice task

This introductory activity practises the skills, understanding and processes required for the major project for this unit. It uses a proverb as a starting point for playbuilding and encourages students to start generating ideas for performance, where they are working with some of the key techniques of this form of theatre. Because it is a practice task done as a whole class, where they work in teams with specific areas of responsibility, students are able to explore possibilities safely and creatively.

Students are to imagine they are a large street/event theatre company with a commission to create a piece of outdoor theatre for the community surrounding their school or their local area. The work is to be based on the proverb: *There is no place like home*. The teacher leads the class in discussion about the following:

- What special issues or themes could be the focus of the play?
- What would be the main idea the class want to communicate to their community audience?
- What symbols, icons or archetypes could they work with that their audience would engage with?

The class is then divided into smaller groups which will each have a specialised area of expertise. The task is for each group to generate a number of ideas for their company to use in their performance. Areas are:

- giant puppets
- banners and posters
- use of fabrics, materials and colour
- masks
- use of music and sound
- costume
- use of the site
- strategies for connecting with the audience.

Each group presents their ideas to the class. The teacher facilitates a discussion about which ideas might be the most practical and the most engaging, given their main idea for the performance. It is also important to discuss possible challenges inherent in the presentations, so that students are starting to think about the project as a whole and what is best for the work, rather than wanting to include too many ideas or too complex suggestions that may not be achievable in performance. Students can reflect on this task in their workbooks in terms of what constraints and issues they feel are the most important when working in this form of theatre. This activity will be a useful reference point for the students' main task for this unit.

Assessment *of learning task*

The following assessment *of* learning task should be given to the students at this point in their learning.

Assessment *of* learning task

The task: out and about

You will work in large groups to create a piece of street/outdoor theatre for an audience of teachers and peers from within their school environment. Each group will select *one* proverb to use as the starting point for street theatre/site-specific theatre AND *one* site that would be most appropriate and interesting to use for staging their play.

Proverbs	Possible sites for performance
• You are what you eat. • Don't judge a book by its cover. • A penny for your thoughts. • Love is blind.	• School canteen, café or dinner hall. • School or local library. • Classroom or corridor. • School quadrangle or balconies. • Large space – like a hall or football field or park. • Another space they think may be suitable within the school.

Groups will spend the next six weeks devising their play and performing it in a location outside the classroom. You will be required to use and apply the techniques and principles of street theatre as you playbuild your work. Throughout the process your teacher will assess you on the three core practices of drama (making, performing and reflecting). You will need to play an active role in all group work, meet deadlines and maintain good records of your practical work in your workbooks.

Assessment criteria

Making the drama

- Offer and contribute imaginative ideas that help create the play.
- Develop ideas in practice through experimentation and collaboration.
- Creatively and effectively respond to the challenges and problems that may arise as the work takes shape.
- Demonstrate your understanding of this form through the effective use of the techniques of street/outdoor theatre.
- Consider the implications of audience and site as you devise your play.

Performing the drama

- Play an active role in the rehearsal and performance process of your group.
- Participate in the performance with commitment, focus and energy appropriate to the work, which engages your audience.
- Support the action and other players at all times during the performance.

Reflecting on the drama

- Reflect effectively on the development of the work throughout the playbuilding process.
- Use your own and the group's reflections to refine the work at key intervals in the devising.
- Reflect on your own contribution and learning at the end of the project.
- Consider areas for future improvement for yourself and the class.

Note to teachers

When using areas of the school that are major traffic areas or areas used for other purposes, it is extremely important that teachers discuss their planning and performance requirements with members of the drama department and school executive. Teachers may need to elect to use the site at specific times and/or control the way the audience and performers access the site for safety reasons. Also consider how other classes and subjects use the particular site. Teachers may need to factor in the school timetable and also what classes or events are positioned around the site at the time you wish to use them (e.g. for noise considerations).

Phase two: constructing phase (about four weeks)

Brainstorming

Each group creates a mindmap of the ideas generated by their chosen proverb. In their groups students discuss:

- What mental images does the proverb conjure up for them?
- What is its intended meaning?
- What new directions could be taken with this proverb?
- What symbols, images and icons could be used to communicate the ideas?
- What could be some interesting dramatic moments that could be explored in your scenario?

Improvisation

The groups now start to create short scenes that capture some of these ideas. These are shared with the class and discussed. Students give each other ideas on how they might develop these ideas further. Allow each group to devise at least two different short scenes. Then they have some variety of possible pathways for their work. Further ideas will be generated with the following assessment *for* learning activity, which is an oral presentation.

The pitch
Each student now creates a creative pitch to give to their group that captures their own ideas for a street theatre performance based on their chosen proverb. Each student completes the following worksheet and includes any additional designs for their presentation. The group then gives feedback to the practitioner about their ideas, their practicalities and merits. Each group then discusses the aspects of each presentation that could be woven together to form their group's play. These could be recorded on cardboard or in students' workbooks for future reference.

Proverbs worksheet

Name:

- Proverb selected:

- Group members:

- Performance site:

- Audience positioning:

- Accepted meaning of proverb:

- The meaning you wish to convey in your play:

- Key images or symbols to be used:

- Ideas for possible scenarios:

- Effects and techniques to be used:

Clarifying the main idea of the piece

By now there are various ideas about what each group could explore in their plays. Now it is time to synthesise those ideas and move the groups to one main interpretation. Each group is to state clearly the main idea they wish to convey to the audience in their play. They then create three tableaux that capture that interpretation.

Focusing on key images and symbols

Each group now considers the key symbols, icons or images they will use in their play. Encourage students to consider first, easily recognisable symbols and then secondly, why each one is important to their main idea. The group also discusses which of these symbols should be heightened, exaggerated or emphasised and why. Their decisions need to be justifiable in terms of the theatrical impact of the idea.

The group could then begin to plan how these key images or symbols could be represented (students draw on their understandings from earlier activities to do this). At the end of this session, make sure students are sharing their decisions with the class as a whole. This enables feedback to be given and new ideas to be offered for consideration.

Developing characters

Each group should give time to creating key characters for their plays and divide into smaller groups to work on different characters who will contribute to the whole piece. This may take a few lessons as students build their ideas and start to make important connections between the ideas that are surfacing as they improvise. Encourage students to use archetypal characters or stock characters that are connected to the underlying idea and purpose of their play and are easily recognisable to their audience. Students should be thinking creatively and devise characters that are larger than life. They also need to consider the dramatic function of each character in the work. Students can present improvised monologues and scenes, perhaps documentary-style (like a nature show), showing the character at work, to generate ideas for characterisation and character relationships. They can also focus on scenes where characters meet or where one character tries to influence another in some way.

Creating the key dramatic moments of the play

Students now consider what will be the basic dramatic moments that will make up their scenarios. Students will create these with the performance site in mind, thinking about how the space itself will be utilised during the scenes. At this point they consider where the action will take place and also where the audience will be positioned. Initially they can work on the basic structure in terms of the *beginning, middle* and *end* of their scenario. Students can share the work they have created by each group creating a large comic strip on butcher's paper or cardboard, showing the moments they have devised so far.

Creating objects and effects

A substantial amount of time will now be devoted to making and constructing the special objects and effects each group wants to use in their play. The teacher would need to facilitate the decision making here, to keep the groups on track. The larger more complicated items will consume more of the groups' time. Each group should try not to be too ambitious. Opting for too many large figures or complicated puppets may take longer to make than is possible. Each group should plan to make no more than two large puppets and/or a few large masks, or even less. The age and capabilities of students will be important for teachers to factor into this part of the creative process. Teachers may want to limit the parameters and choices for younger students.

There are many different ways to construct masks, giant puppets and objects. There are useful notes in *Engineers of the Imagination: Welfare State Handbook* (Coult and Kershaw 1999, pp.60–79). In addition, there are many good websites available on the internet showing how to make puppets and masks for performances, parades and processions. Essentially students will be constructing large puppets using a basic pole or backpack design. Masks can be made quickly and effectively out of papier-mâché.

In designing and then making their puppets, banners or masks, students will need to consider:

- Overall look of the object – what is to be emphasised and why?
- How weight is managed/distributed in the design, e.g. how many people will be needed to operate the puppet or mask? How easy will it be to move with it?
- The construction of the object – what materials? Where are the movable joints? What areas need to be strengthened/reinforced? How?
- Will there be any triggers or moveable mechanisms on the puppet or mask? If groups are short of time might this be too difficult?
- What materials, fabrics and colours will be used?
- How will the group manage this part of the project: e.g. time, space and responsibilities?

The teacher will need to consider:

- Materials required – it is important to use light-weight, inexpensive, easy-to-purchase and -manage materials. Recycled paper, fabric, bamboo, string are all useful items. The teacher needs to consider how durable the materials are. Also, how will students be monitored in their use of materials?
- Space and time – where will the students work? For how long? Where will the objects be stored while they work on them? How can the students test out and experiment with their objects after the making phase is over?
- Fast and effective group work will be necessary for this phase of the process.
- Safety of students – it is critical in the making and performing phases that teachers ensure students work safely in terms of using materials and also carrying and manipulating their large puppets or masks. Teachers will need to ensure there is enough space for students to experiment and students are not required to lift or carry objects for lengthy periods or in difficult positions. Teachers have a duty of care to ensure safe practices at all times.
- How will the students experiment and get used to their object? How does it move? What issues become important when learning to manipulate their puppet/mask? What effect does their puppet/mask have on the drama itself and the atmosphere created?

Phase three: structuring phase (about one week)

It is important to give students time to put all the elements together as effectively as possible and to have enough time to practise using the objects and effects they have created. While they are structuring their plays they are also clarifying the *weave* of their work by discovering how their ideas 'gel' together and how to resolve issues such as use of space, timing and manipulation of objects and materials. Students will need to consider entrances and exits, the positioning of the audience, sound and visibility issues. The links they create will need to ensure the momentum of performance is sustained and their audience remains engaged at all times. At this point students should consider what kind of atmosphere and tension are created in the work. They may need to devise small scenes to link some of their earlier work. Students will need to consider how they connect with the audience and at which points in the dramatic structure.

Once the shape and structure of the work is decided and clear to all group members, each group should construct a map of their scenario, using the template headings shown in Figure 5.2.

Dramatic moment	Description/ what is happening	How will this be conveyed?	Who is involved?	Additional items needed	Music

Figure 5.2 Constructing a map

Production elements should be kept to a minimum and be mostly symbolic rather than realistic. Groups should make key decisions about costuming and make-up. They should think about exaggerated styles and colours, and how they add to the larger-than-life effect of the performance.

Phase four: performative phase (about one week)

In the final phase of the playbuilding students polish their work and, where possible, rehearse in the site with the objects and effects they have made. They should be focusing on smooth transitions, effective manipulation of the puppets, masks, fabrics and banners, audibility of dialogue, clarity of characterisation, strong exaggerated acting styles and the creation and maintenance of dramatic tension and atmosphere throughout their play. Students should anticipate and plan how their audience will move or be positioned in the site and also they should anticipate and discuss any problems that might arise. Students may need to do some running repairs on some of their constructed items, as they may have been weakened while the group rehearses. Prior to performance it is good to do a quick check of all levers, connections, straps and sewing, to see if they are strong enough for the performance.

The groups of students perform their plays in their chosen site. It may not be possible to stage them all at once, particularly if the site is in use for other purposes. The performances could happen perhaps over a series of lunchtimes or days. While each group performs, the other classmates should be assisting with production elements or monitoring the audience or helping in other ways (such as removing larger items from the space when they are no longer needed). In staging outdoor performances weather is a key factor. Students need to be able to perform smoothly and safely (sometimes windy conditions prohibit a performance if using large puppets or banners).

Reflecting on the playbuilding

Students will have been reflecting regularly upon the ideas and work as they emerge throughout the whole unit. It is important they understand that good creative processes rely on a strong reflective approach to help generate ideas and material. Time should be devoted to debriefing after the performance and giving students various opportunities and ways in which to reflect on the creative process, the performance event and its impact, as well as their own contribution to the work. Students should be encouraged to both speak and write about their experiences and consider which parts of the playbuilding process they found challenging and possible ways they could improve on in future projects. Students should reflect back to some of their earlier lessons and consider how their piece of outdoor street theatre connected to the ideas, practices and examples they learned about at the start of the unit. A final discussion could be about what students have learned about this form of drama from the process of making their own piece of street theatre.

Chapter 6

Level 3: experienced playbuilders

Teaching considerations for experienced playbuilders

In level 3-based playbuilding, theme-, character- and location-devised plays scaffold upon levels 1 and 2 learning as experienced playbuilders build on their previous units of work. In level 3 the teacher introduces sophisticated playbuilding concepts to the students and initially guides and facilitates the experienced playbuilders until they grasp the concepts of their playbuilding project. Reflective and evaluative strategies are implicitly embedded in all the units of work as students are constantly interpreting and examining the learning that is taking place in each project.

The teaching strategies for experienced playbuilders extend the depth and breadth of their skills, knowledge and understanding of how to collaboratively create their own plays. The strategies are more advanced in the way that they are taught on the classroom floor, and it is important for the teacher to be fluid and instinctive in their approach as every project at this level will generate its own working processes. A strong level-3 playbuilding experience should provide challenging teaching strategies that provoke a mature imaginative response.

Learner profile

Students who undertake level 3-based playbuilding have engaged in numerous playbuilding projects during their drama learning. These students have a mature approach to extending their making, performing and reflecting, and they will be highly skilled in their knowledge and understanding of playbuilding processes, and will be able to grasp the importance of exploring starting points outside of the realm of their own experience.

THEME-BASED PLAYBUILDING: GETTING POLITICAL

Unit description

In this unit of work students explore and perform complex political themes; this challenges and deepens the playbuilder's drama learning. The theme is chosen by the whole class from a current political situation such as consumerism, the environment, stem cell research. This type of playbuilding highlights the sometimes controversial nature of the performing arts contribution to society's discourses.

How long?

The suggested timeline is 10 weeks based on 4 × 50-minute lessons a week.

Phase one: generative phase (about one week)

How to choose a theme from a current political issue

The process of deciding on a theme should take about a week. As the playbuilding will be examining and dramatically debating a point in question, *theme* will be referred to as *issue* in this project. As discussed in Chapter 3, the teacher should start each class with appropriate voice and body warm-ups.

A suggested opening discussion to have with experienced playbuilders could be:

> The type of work you are going to undertake will provide you with an opportunity to playbuild around an issue that you might not normally think can be used for playbuilding. In this playbuilding project we will dramatically explore a current political issue. By political I mean the public affairs of a nation and its government and how they affect our lives. For example, our government provides us with rules and regulations to maintain and safeguard the environment.

- Why do they do this?
- Do you think they do this successfully?
- What could they do differently?
- Why would an audience want to see a play about such an issue?
- Can anyone name a current issue of interest to them?
- What possibilities do your issues have for playbuilding?
- How do you go about creating a political play as a whole class?

From this discussion the class will have an initial understanding of the task they are undertaking and why they are undertaking it. Students should record the discussion in their workbooks, writing their own definitions and examples of what *political* means to them. Over about two days, students create a mindmap of current political issues (see Figure 6.1).

Once the mindmap has been completed the whole class discusses the issues it has raised. Students form groups from their particular choices. They make and perform an improvisation that persuades their peers that their ideas are the most dramatically interesting. The class votes on the issue for their playbuilding project. There will usually be a few students who do not feel sure about the outcome of this vote and it is important for the teacher to reassure them that their voices will be heard throughout the process.

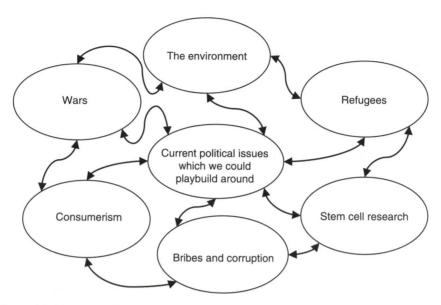

Figure 6.1 Mindmap of current political issues

Phase two: constructing phase (about one week)

In this hypothetical situation the students have chosen the issue of *the environment*. The teacher and the students must record all future activities so that there is a performance record to draw on when creating the final dramatic structure.

Assessment of learning task

The class are given an assessment *of* learning task and discuss its content and purpose.

Assessment *of* learning task

As a whole class you are all going to create a political playbuilding project around the issue you have all decided upon. Then, in small groups, but coming back together at certain points as a whole class, make and perform a play that has a wide range of different viewpoints and challenges your audience to think about the intended message. The assessment will take into account how well you develop your playbuilding issue using pertinent dramatic conventions, techniques and performance styles.

Conditions
- 10 weeks to devise the play.
- Elements of production should be used to enhance the staging of the play.
- Outside-of-class rehearsals will be held in the last two weeks.
- The play should be 50–60 minutes in length and will be performed to a public audience.

You will be assessed individually using the following criteria.
Your contribution to:

Making the drama
- researching the issue;
- using improvisation techniques to examine the research;
- integrating the polished improvisations into the playbuilding;
- integrating differing viewpoints into the playbuilding;
- structuring the playbuilding theatrically;

Performing the drama
- managing the dramatic conventions, techniques and performance styles creatively;
- an innovative production that evokes a powerful actor/audience response;

Reflecting on the drama
- continuously engaging with the collaboration process;
- recognising dramatic problems and solving them in the group;
- critically reflecting on your own work and the work of others in your group;
- a detailed individual workbook of your processes which is to be handed in a week after the final performance.

To begin with the students organise themselves into groups of 5–6. These groups are initial improvising groups. Each group is given a balloon and told that it represents the environment. They must look after the balloon by keeping it constantly in the air. They are not allowed to hold the balloon, the balloon must not hit any other object other than their own bodies because if it does a small environmental disaster occurs – *the student who touched the balloon is eliminated*. The groups start playing the activity, and the teacher adds more elimination rules:

- The balloon cannot touch anyone's arms or hands.
- Now the balloon can only touch legs and feet, or heads.
- Finally, the balloon can only touch heads.

As the extra rules are added, all other rules still apply, making the game progressively harder, especially as students are eliminated. When the game is finished the class comes together for a discussion:

- How did the game feel after the rules were added?
- How did it feel when members of the group were eliminated?

The teacher discusses the connection to their issue:

Let's imagine that the balloon is a symbol for the environment, the individual groups represent the general populace and the rules represent policies that affect our environment. As you discovered, the rules/policies became harder and more frustrating through the activity. Why?

- How do the activities relate to your issue?

- Describe the dramatic structure of the activity.
- How would you change the activity to make it into a scene?
- What research do you need to do now?

All students, individually, in pairs or in groups should undertake relevant research. They could find out why and how certain government bodies have made decisions about the environment now and in the past, or examine case studies such as a car manufacturer's environmental mission statement, or even contact local environmental groups for their opinions. This means that the students will undertake research in areas such as:

- print media;
- television programmes;
- documentaries;
- internet sites such as the 'Intelligence2' website that provide a forum for debate on political issues of the day;
- writing to and/or creating questionnaires for companies, political parties and individuals.

This type of research continues throughout the whole unit of work.

Incorporating different viewpoints into scenes

During phase two the teacher introduces the importance of incorporating different viewpoints, both public and private, into the developing scenes as the challenge for the class is to engage their audience in a piece of theatre that makes them think deeply about the political issue.

This teaching strategy explores different viewpoints and is based on the dynamics of pull and push in improvisations; it encourages students to become aware of the importance of dramatic contradictions while developing scenes and roles with different viewpoints:

- Working in pairs students face each other; they bend their knees and look into one another's eyes. Slowly they both raise their right arm and swing it over their heads grasping their partner by the right forearm. When this is done they slowly raise their left arm and swing it over their heads grasping their partner's left forearm. The students, maintaining a firm grip of each others' forearms, then slowly pull and lean back testing their partnership balance. The teacher asks the pairs to start rotating their arms, first right then left. This provides a pushing of the body while the pairs simultaneously pull back to keep their balance. Sustaining the same rhythm and balance, the students discuss the chosen issue and its differing viewpoints. To extend this activity the students could explore it while taking on different roles with different attitudes to the issue.
- All pairs provide feedback to the class on their discussions and the difficulties of pulling and pushing while discussing.
- The teacher describes how an activity like this could be used in the playbuilding. For example, the opening of the play could be a scene with all students pulling and pushing while using pertinent dialogue to introduce the push and pull of their political issue.

Students could develop this improvisation by creating diverse body shapes that use the concept of push and pull (Murray 2003).

Phase three: structuring phase [first part] (about three weeks)

Structuring is divided into two parts for ease of teaching. The first part focuses on developing scenes.

Groupings

To begin phase three the class is divided into groups of 6–8 students. Choosing the groups is done by the teacher in consultation with the students. These groups can remain the same during the entire process or groups can develop a scene and then form other groupings to create another scene. It is important to remind the students that the *whole class* is creating one playbuilding project, and at certain learning points throughout this process these groups will come back together as a *class ensemble* and link and integrate their scenes.

> **Handy hint . . .**
> *These class ensemble points are indicated throughout the process.*

Making scenes

All groups must negotiate the aspect of the issue they are going to develop into a scene so that there is minimal overlapping; this may mean that a group takes one viewpoint while another focuses on the alternative viewpoint. For example, one group could focus on fossil fuels, another on alternative fuels, another on petrol-based cars, and another on non-polluting transport in an economy.

Each group is given a different dramatic structure that they must manipulate and use to initially develop a scene. They should be reminded that their research must somehow be incorporated into this scene.

Group 1:

- Masked and unmasked characters.
- Slow motion.

Group 2:

- Movement and music.
- Material.

Group 3:

- Soundscapes which create atmosphere and tension.
- The soundscape should be set in a location: e.g. a city street, a rainforest.

Group 4:

- An image that depicts both sides of the argument.
- The image should be created as theatre in the round, as it will be viewed from a 360° angle so that the class can see all the theatrical possibilities.

Once the groups have some basic structure they should keep extending these scenes until they have a 3–5-minute rehearsed scene to perform to their peers for dramatic critiquing. Once a scene has been developed, the groups should be asked to take another area of research and create another scene by choosing from the following drama structures:

- creating a public policy machine;
- creating an orchestra of issues;
- creating an international slow motion tug-of-war;
- creating a race with chairs demonstrating an environmental dilemma;
- using a symbol as the focus of the scene;
- using different performance styles.

When each group has one or two structured scenes and the class has peer critiqued them, each group could be asked to create any scene they wish using any performance style. Sometimes groups can come up with amazing scenes at this point in their learning, but other groups will flounder with such little direction and it may be necessary to remind them of the activities they have previously explored such as with the *balloons,* or *pull and push* that have potential for scene creation.

While creating all their scenes it is important to remind the groups to use their research; for example they could:

- turn their research into dialogue between characters/roles or inanimate objects;
- personify their research;
- select an object from the research and explore the different ways the object could be used in a scene;
- project visual images or pertinent words from the research as a backdrop to scenes.

Critiquing the scenes

After one and a half weeks of rehearsing the whole class comes back together as an ensemble to critique the developing scenes again. In critiquing the different scenes the whole class should examine how they have incorporated the elements of drama. For example, questions about adding or changing the emotional intensity of a scene, adding tension or a dilemma to a scene, magnifying one aspect of a scene and diminishing another, are all pertinent. The critiquing must also make sure the scenes show a number of viewpoints.

Groups should be given a week to incorporate this critiquing; this could be an assessment *for* learning activity.

- In groups students are to develop their rehearsed scene incorporating the refinements decided upon by the whole class. All students must record their scene in their workbooks.

Each group would perform their revised scene using the appropriate techniques and conventions and the teacher would monitor their work. Once this process has been undertaken these scenes will be only briefly revisited in the next two weeks as it is now time to start creating a firm structure around the playbuilding.

Phase three: structuring phase [second part] (about two and a half weeks)

In this second structuring phase the class finds a title for their play and develops a dramatic structure through the exploration of linkings and metaphoric devising. The questions that need to be asked in the second part of phase three are:

- Where are you heading?
- Why are you heading there?
- What message do you want to give to your audience?

Once these questions have been discussed the following can be asked:

- What dramatic structure do you need to create?
- What should you call your play?

Finding a title

The class have to find a title for their play that demonstrates the differing viewpoints. This gives their playbuilding a solid dramatic focus. They should brainstorm their ideas. For example, a playbuilding piece that deals with the environment could be titled *The Environment – Who Cares?*

Metaphor and linkings

As discussed in Chapter 3, creating a metaphor is a way of structuring the scenes and creating new contexts and meanings for the issues being explored. To think of an appropriate metaphor and to incorporate it as part of the dramatic structure can take up to a couple of weeks. A dramatically dynamic metaphor can also provide most of the linkings for the play.

The whole class brainstorms what metaphors could be appropriate for their intended message and record this in their workbooks. If the students are not sure about the purpose and function of a dramatic metaphor the teacher could give a couple of suggestions:

> As a whole class you are going to become the *Gods of the Environment*. The Gods are a metaphor for power and control over your environment. The performance style of chorus will be used by the Gods to structure and link the scenes. Don't forget chorus is a collection of roles or characters that act in unison, almost as one person. They usually speak together in one voice and move together with similar or exactly the same actions.

Using their research the whole class improvises small scenes where they act as a chorus of Gods of the Environment. The Gods could:

- comment on and predict the dramatic action of the different scenes;
- become a unified narrator of the scenes, telling the audience their story;
- split into two groups with both sides presenting opposing viewpoints of issues.

The whole class discusses whether this metaphor is appropriate and how it might be theatrically used to link scenes together and to engage their audience. If they are not sure that the metaphor is workable they should explore another, for example the teacher could adapt and manipulate Rudolf Laban's movement techniques to help the class create and develop a movement piece that transforms their bodies into the weather.

> *Handy hint . . .*
> *A good textbook to gain knowledge and skills in the Laban technique is J. Newlove's* Laban for Actors and Dancers: Putting Laban's Movement Theory into Practice *(1993).*

The teacher explains:

> You are going to explore movement techniques to become weather patterns. This whole-class physicalised movement will be a dramatic metaphor for weather and its influence on the environment. Different metaphoric movement pieces could be used to link scenes and could be enhanced by creating visual images of the environment projected onto a backdrop behind the action. Music could be added if appropriate.

The class is asked to travel around the space becoming heavy in their movements then light in their movements. They are to travel fast then slow; rise up and then lower their bodies down; advance to the centre of the room by the most direct route, then retreat by the most indirect route.

The teacher explains that they have been exploring the basic motions of *weight, time* and *space.* These are broken up into:

- weight which is strong and heavy or light and fine movements;
- time which is jerky and sudden or smooth and sustained movements;
- space which is direct movements using as little space as possible and/or flexible movements using as much space as possible.

To reiterate these basic motions the teacher asks all the class to drop to the floor in a strong, direct and sudden manner. They must remain where they are for a few seconds and then come up in a light, flexible and sustained manner. The class discuss how movement is used as a tool to enhance the process of communication in performance and how they could incorporate these basic motions of weight, time and space to create a movement metaphor of weather.

From this exploration the teacher asks the whole class to create a group kinaesthetic movement piece by developing a:

- punching action (strong, sudden and direct) to become a destructive storm;
- slashing action (strong, sudden and flexible) to become an aggressive rain;
- floating action (light, sustained and flexible) to become clouds;
- flicking action (light, sudden and flexible) to become small gusts of wind;
- manipulating weight, time and space in any way they see fit.

If time permitted the whole class could spend a number of lessons exploring all of Laban's different types of *effort actions*, but the techniques given here are to help the class experiment with wordless metaphoric messages, and as such the students do not need to develop an in-depth understanding of this dance/drama genre.

Once a decision has been made on what metaphor to use, the whole class will work as an ensemble, structuring and linking the scenes that have been developed so far.

Phase four: performative phase (about two and a half weeks)

During phase four the teacher facilitates the students' developing performative work. They monitor whole-class work and the individual groups, helping them solve problems and create dramatic structures that have a clear theatrical intention. The types of difficulties that arise during the process are:

- students not trusting the research to have a dramatic voice;
- incorporating the research into the scenes;
- one viewpoint of the issue totally overriding another;
- finding a metaphor and creating a whole-class structure;
- group dynamics;
- keeping to timelines.

Teaching strategies to solve and manage these difficulties include:

- using the talking circle to find out everybody's point of view which enhances the collaborative learning;
- exploring the nexus of the actor–audience relationship in relation to political theatre;
- reviewing the concept of pull and push in the scenes;
- discussing what scenes lack research and incorporate this;
- rehearsing and refining the first scenes so that they are polished;
- reviewing what scenes show what viewpoint and deciding where they should go in the structure;
- discussing what other scenes need to be developed from the research and the students' own stories, and helping the groups to devise and polish these;
- refining roles and characters;
- refining the dramatic structure including metaphor and linkings;

- timing the play so that it runs for 50–60 minutes;
- rehearsing and refining the performance.

All the elements of production are incorporated into this playbuilding project. This means that the class must discuss and decide how they wish to costume the many roles they will most probably be taking on. For example, would it be better for all students to be in black and use such things as scarves and hats to delineate one role from another, or if time permits, would it be more appropriate to have costume changes. They will also need to discuss what type of set, lights, and sound effects are appropriate to the play given its overriding metaphor. Finally it would be very useful for the class to create a poster and programme as this activity can help them synthesise their knowledge of how they have structured their play and what the overriding message is to their audience.

The whole class could perform the play several times to the general public. This gives them the opportunity to experience the nature of repertory theatre. After the class has performed the play they should discuss their work and write reflections and evaluations in their workbooks about the merits or otherwise of this project and what they could apply to their next unit of drama work.

CHARACTER-BASED PLAYBUILDING: SUSTAINING CHARACTERS IN THE STYLE OF REALISM

Unit description

In this unit of work students explore the performance style of realism in conjunction with developing and sustaining a single character within their group's playbuilding project. Level 3 character-based playbuilding requires careful development and construction so that all the dramatic components of a character are developed in conjunction with the devising. For experienced playbuilders, character-based playbuilding can be firmly based on the performance style of realism; realism scaffolds upon level 2's physical approach to developing and sustaining character.

How long?

Suggested timeline is 8 weeks based on 4 × 50-minute lessons a week.

Phase one: generative phase (about one week)

The unit of work begins by asking the class what realism in the theatre means to them and how it might differ from realism in films or television programmes. The teacher may also synthesise the students' discussion by giving a definition such as:

> Realism is a performance style based in truth. It requires you to build a realistic character profile both physically and physiologically. All the conventions and techniques of realism guide the character through the play so that the characterisation does not become clichéd.

From these initial discussions the teacher explains that in this first week they are going to explore acting techniques to help them develop realistic characters and these techniques will be applied in a playbuilding project that focuses on the performance style of realism.

Students are asked to recall and share with the class different personal experiences and the associated emotions such as:

- being deeply infatuated with someone
- feeling inspired
- being afraid;

and contrasting emotions such as:

- being confident versus fearful
- feeling hopeful versus despairing
- being sad versus happy.

Discussion follows about the importance of creating believable emotions when developing characters, and the next teaching strategy is designed to help students begin this process.

Students find their own place in the classroom and listen to the following story. They must imagine that it is a real situation. As the story is being told they should become the character and immerse themselves in the emotions:

> You feel fantastic, you could dance for joy – after a couple of years of hard work you have just won a most prestigious prize for a project you developed. Now you and your partner can finally afford to get married and buy your dream home, and your partner's previous girl/boyfriend, who always intimidated you, has left to live overseas. All this is the best personal news you have had in months. You rush over to your partner's home to tell him/her your news and as you arrive you see his/her previous girl/boyfriend leave. You are shocked and momentarily feel you could kill them both for their perceived deceitful behaviour.

> **Handy hint . . .**
> *Moni Yakim's textbook* Creating a Character *(1990) is useful to assist with developing these types of stories.*

After the class have listened to the story they are asked to find a space in the room and individually improvise the scene thinking about the emotions that the story elicits for them, and what emotions are concealed or obvious and why. The following are examples of questions that are asked after the improvisation and can also be answered in the students' workbooks:

- Would anyone like to share the emotions their character went through?
- What was concealed or obvious and why?
- Were there contrasting emotions?

- Did anyone place their character in a specific location at a specific time? If so, how did this impact on the improvisations?
- What did your character want to achieve? In other words, was there an objective(s)?
- Did your character reach this objective(s)?
- What were the obstacle(s) in the way?
- What aspect of this improvisation was truthful and why?
- Would anyone care to show their improvisation to the rest of the class?

A student is asked to perform their improvisation and afterwards the class analyses that character's emotions in relation to the situation, time, location, and his or her objectives and obstacles. This improvisation would most probably be a good example of the fourth wall, which is the invisible wall between actors and the audience, and this concept could be discussed.

Class notes are given to clarify the terminology of the acting techniques and there is discussion that this knowledge will be applied to their group plays in the forthcoming weeks.

Acting techniques

- Objective(s) is(are) the character's principal quest, which the actor assumes. Everything on stage must be seen as a character pursuing objectives with a strong motivation to do so.
- No objective can be achieved simply by yourself.
- There are obstacles to pursuing objectives, sometimes these obstacles prevent a character pursuing or achieving an objective. This can make a drama very powerful.
- A character's emotions relate directly to their objectives as well as to how they feel about the obstacles.
- Tactics are used by a character to achieve objectives and overcome the obstacles. Tactics will be explored in greater depth later on in the unit of work.
- Situation, time and location are vital components out of which all realistic plays are built.
- The fourth wall is the invisible line between the actors and the audience.
- Initial questions to ask as you develop a character:
  Who am I?

  ○ What is my objective(s) and what motivates me?
  ○ What obstacle(s) is stopping me gaining my objective(s)?
  ○ How can I overcome my obstacle(s)?
  ○ What should be my tactics?
  ○ What are my emotions?
  ○ What are the situation, time and location and how do they impact on my objective?

Handy hint . . .
Throughout this unit of work students could refer to Bella Merlin's textbook Konstantin Stanislavsky *(2003) to expand their knowledge of realism.*

The purpose and function of an independent activity

The next teaching strategy helps students to realise the importance of connecting spontaneous psychological action to a moment in time. When students are developing realistic characters they sometimes find it hard to think of something purposeful for their character to do in a given situation. The following teaching strategy allows students to explore the importance of small physical actions in a scene which contribute to the overall dramatic meaning.

The teacher discusses with the class:

> An independent activity is a technique an actor explores, generally with a small prop, to help develop their character's psychological and physical worlds. The small prop could be a comb, nail polish, soap, remote control, anything that can impact on the action. The props are used to connect characters' emotions to the moment when they make a physical and psychological point about a given situation. Through the rehearsal process an actor may explore a number of independent activities for their character, some of which will be discarded, others of which will be developed and carried through to help the character pursue their objectives.

The teacher asks the class to walk around the room. At a given signal all the students freeze and listen and react to the instructions. Each improvisation is 5–10 seconds long and is followed by questions.

> You are brushing your teeth because you are getting ready to go to out to a party. You can't wait to get to this party as you really fancy the host. Your flatmate comes downstairs ready to go to the same party; she/he says she/he is just off to meet this person you have been thinking about. React to this situation using your toothbrush as an independent object that responds to your feelings.

The teacher asks a number of students:

- What did you do with the toothbrush to physically demonstrate what you felt?
- How did the toothbrush impact on the scene?
- What does your reaction with the toothbrush say about your improvised character?
- What was your character's objective, obstacle, emotions?
- What were the situation, time and location?
- What elements of realism did you observe in your own spontaneous improvisation?

The class explores another spontaneous improvisation to help consolidate the learning:

You are cutting up carrots in your kitchen. Your partner is late as usual. You have a feeling that she/he has been seeing someone else. She/he comes into the kitchen. What do you say and do?

The teacher asks a number of students to show their improvisations and a discussion ensues on how the carrot, knife and the kitchen itself may have become an independent activity to vent a character's feelings about the situation.

Putting it all together with a bare script

The students are now asked to apply their learning from all these realistic acting techniques into a rehearsed improvisation. This is an assessment *for* learning activity so that the teacher can observe what students have practically understood and how they apply their understanding. The following activity would take about two to three lessons.

In pairs the students are asked to read small bare scripts that the teacher has constructed. For example:

A: No.
B: I thought you might.
A: Oh.
B: Great.

Each pair is given a different bare script and the following instructions:

> Bare script activity
> Read the attached bare script with your partner and discuss, improvise and write down in your workbooks the following:
>
> - Who are you both? For example age, profession and relationships.
> - What is the situation?
> - What is the time and location of your scene?
> - What are your characters' objectives in the scene; remember a character does not always achieve their objectives.
> - What are your characters' emotions? Are they contrasting emotions, obvious or concealed?
> - Does the dialogue have subtext, if so what is it?
> - What are your physical actions? Remember that you, the actor, have to know what your character is doing exactly, and at every moment in the scene.
> - Does your character have a prop that functions as an independent activity? (Please make sure that at least one character has an independent activity somewhere during the scene.)
> - A restriction on this improvisation is that you are not allowed to add any more dialogue. You must make sense of the scene from the bare script dialogue.

The teacher explains to the class that this rehearsed improvisation needs to be about a minute long and to incorporate the fourth wall concept. The students should costume their characters simply, and use the actual prop they chose for their independent activity.

The class performs the bare scripts and discusses the purpose and function of the realistic acting techniques, how successful they were, and how they can be applied when developing a character in their forthcoming playbuilding project.

Actable objectives

Students can find it hard to think of actable objectives. Giving them an initial list of simple objectives for the above task can be helpful. They can also add to this worksheet over the forthcoming character-based playbuilding unit of work. A starting list of actable objectives that can be achieved physically and verbally is as follows:

To:

Accuse	Agree	Advise	Annoy	Beg
Blame	Boss	Cling	Confess	Charm
Confront	Control	Dismiss	Dominate	Deceive
Encourage	Entertain	Flatter	Guide	Greet
Harass	Humiliate	Ignore	Lie	Laugh
Mock	Mimic	Mislead	Order	Pamper
Pester	Quiz	Resist	Scare	Sooth
Seduce	Tempt	Terrify	Upset	Warn
Yell	Yield			

or

To avoid the answer	To challenge authority	To cover up my guilt
To demand recognition	To mislead the enemy	To pester others
To praise others	To create gloom	To win admirers.

> *Handy hint . . .*
> *The class could also create their own lists of character emotions, situations, times, location and independent activities while playbuilding.*

Phase two: constructing phase (about one week)

Based on the class's initial knowledge and understanding of the generative phase the teacher asks the class to sit in a circle and write a couple of sentences in their workbook on what *realism in a devised play* means to them. The class shares their ideas and playbuilding groups are then formed

Groupings

Groups of 4–6 mixed-ability students.

Assessment of learning task

An assessment *of* learning task that caters for mixed-ability students is handed out.

Assessment *of* learning task

Character playbuilding based on the performance style of realism
Each student will collaborate with a group in devising a play based on the performance style of realism. Each student is to develop a single character in this play that will demonstrate an understanding and application of realistic acting techniques. Your devised play will be 8–12 minutes long. Your group is to choose one of these starting points as a stimulus to develop your dramatic ideas:

- a life of luxury and a monastic existence
- betwixt and between
- entangled with the shadows
- landscapes
- the missing question
- the past is abolished
- today is Wednesday.

Your playbuilding must actively demonstrate the elements of drama, which are situation, roles, characters and relationships, are directed by focus and driven by tension and made explicit in moment, time and location through the media of language and movement to create mood and symbols which together create dramatic meaning, audience engagement and truthful characterisation.

Workbook
Your workbook will be used to record, research, reflect and evaluate your characterisation process in the devised play as well as discussing how your process work relates to the elements of drama. At the end of the project each student will write a 500- or 800-word report on the whole process. They will show their teacher their draft work at times mutually decided upon; this means that you need to set your own learning goals:

- I have chosen to write a 500- or 800-word report (delete one).
- I will show my teacher the work, to check my progress on the following dates:
  First date: _____
  Second date: _____

Criteria for assessment
You will be assessed individually on the following criteria for the three areas – workbook, elements of drama, and adopting and sustaining a realistic character.

- excellent
- high
- substantial
- satisfactory
- elementary.

The teacher reiterates that the acting techniques from the previous phase need to be applied to this task and that further techniques will be introduced to help every group to develop their character within the performance style of realism.

During the next couple of lessons it is important to run warm-ups that enhance realistic acting techniques such as vocal warm-ups that free the natural voice, or sense and memory, imagination and physical warm-ups. These should take about ten minutes, and groups should then spend the rest of the lessons in a peer learning context that will also include deciding what to research for their developing story.

Phase three: structuring phase [first part] (about two weeks)

Structuring is divided into two parts for ease of teaching. The first part focuses on developing realistic acting techniques.

Teaching strategies for the whole class

It is beneficial to teach the whole class the following two acting techniques, *playing tactics* and *character and change*, as these techniques scaffold upon their previous learning and can help all students develop a dramatic depth to their scene work. For example, the teacher explains the importance of playing tactics while developing realistic characters.

> Characters pursue their objectives by employing tactics. You explore tactics psychologically and through your voice, actions and physicality. Tactics can be divided by those who threaten and those who persuade. For example, glaring at someone else can be a threatening tactic, or breaking into a smile a persuasive tactic. When playing tactics be truthful, do not overact, but find that middle ground. Tactics can help make your acting real.
>
> Here are lists of some tactics that characters use. In your group, experiment with these as well as any others that are pertinent to your developing scenes and discuss the effect and consequences of the tactics and the associated emotions.

When the teacher gives the groups the following lists, she/he reminds them about safety procedures such as never truly hitting another student or bringing verbal personal relationships into these activities.

To threaten:

- frighten the other character;
- make the other character cry;
- intimidate the other character;
- make the other character listen to you;
- make the other character worried about you;
- make the other character feel humiliated.

To persuade:

- make the other character laugh at or with you;
- make the other character proud of you or themselves;
- make the other character warm to you;
- encourage the other character;
- make the other character happy;
- inspire the other character.

When the students have experimented with this they must attempt to apply it to their scene work.

Characters and change

Another whole-class teaching strategy is to introduce the notion of character and change (Greig 2005). The teacher explains:

> Change operates at all levels of human experience; every moment in the scenes in your devised play is about change and it happens on any number of levels. A character can change externally or internally and one change can often affect another. For example, if a character's health deteriorates this might affect their mood, or if a character's religious belief changes this might affect their personal and public allegiances.

Groups should brainstorm their character's external and internal changes and discuss how one might affect the other in the play. The teacher helps the groups by outlining some of the main changes characters go through. For example, working with the group, they could come up with an initial list:

External character change	Internal character change
Wealth	Passions
Allegiances	Beliefs
Friends	Views
Circumstances	Mind
Location	Heart
Health	Mood

From this brainstorming ask the students to:

- find the changes in their characters;
- make sure they are incorporated into their playbuilding scenes;
- and, if they wish, each group could create a character blog to explore the possibilities of how characters change.

Teaching strategies for individual groups

The following types of acting techniques can be taught to groups at different times mutually agreed on. This means the group sets their own learning goals. These techniques are explored through discussion and improvisation, and recorded and reflected in the workbook.

- Each member of the group is asked to find psychological and physical answers to the fundamental character's questions of who, where, when, what and how, and to share this with each other.
- The teacher revises the concept of independent activities and extends this into exploring a character's pace and rhythm. The pace is the speed at which a character's action is performed and the rhythm is the intensity with which the action is performed. For example, the pace is the speed of opening a letter and the rhythm is the emotional degree of opening a letter.
- Students detail what their character is doing (physical action) and thinking (text and subtext) at every scenic moment in the play and share this with their group.
- Each group must demonstrate to the teacher how they are applying their research to the storyline.

During this phase the class are working as individual groups but must also show their developing scenes to each other and the teacher for regular feedback. The talking circle is also a non-threatening way to give feedback in these circumstances. If students are left to their own devices for too long they can easily go off track.

> **Handy hint . . .**
> Remind students to re-examine their acting techniques from the first week's improvisations and apply the lessons in this playbuilding project.

Phase three: structuring phase [second part] (about two and half weeks)

Storyline

It is important to monitor how each group's storyline is developing. If groups are having problems the following teaching strategies are useful:

- Groups create a mindmap about their ideas and write one or two simple paragraphs about the developing storyline.
- Groups use and manipulate an existing story, but need to be reminded that the existing story is only a structure and they should embellish the original story to suit their ideas.
- Groups decide on a location for their story. Once they have chosen a location they develop characters that are dramatically affected by it.

Once the storylines have some basic structure all the groups need to understand how to turn a storyline into a plot.

Developing scenes and plot

The teacher explains:

The definition of a plot is the arrangements of the incidents in the story. A plot can be simple, complex or cyclic and progress in different ways such as:

- beginning, middle and end;
- end, beginning, middle, and epilogue;
- prologue, beginning, juxtaposing middle scenes and end;
- or any other way that enhances your ideas.

The incidents in the plot can be thought of as scenes and create one dominating idea for the audience. These scenic incidents must develop all the characters' relationships within the given situation.

The teacher asks one group to write their story down on the whiteboard. Three sentences would suffice. This group has created a play about a sporting organisation and the starting point they chose was *Entangled with the shadows*. For example:

- A leader of a sporting organisation is trying to manipulate his/her team to commit acts of dishonesty. Some members of the team disagree with this approach but are concerned about losing the prestige of belonging to this sports organisation. A crime war ensues between competing sports personnel.

From this storyline the class discusses what would be the most interesting scenes and plotline and they create a graph. This graph has the characteristics of a cyclic plot.

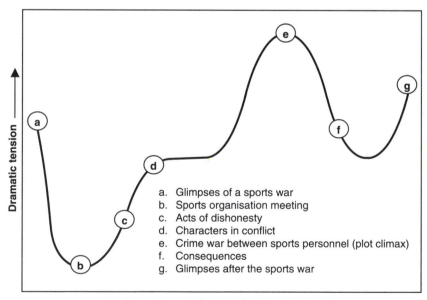

a. Glimpses of a sports war
b. Sports organisation meeting
c. Acts of dishonesty
d. Characters in conflict
e. Crime war between sports personnel (plot climax)
f. Consequences
g. Glimpses after the sports war

a–g = Arrangement of scenic incidents in the plot

Figure 6.2 Development of scenes and plot from the storyline

Groups are asked to work on applying these strategies and to refer back to the elements of drama to visualise if their plot is developing dynamically.

Creating complexity in the plot

Once the groups have developed their storyline in conjunction with the plot the teacher could introduce further strategies that may enhance their character work such as:

- changing the focus from one character to another to present different viewpoints;
- creating scenes within scenes that allow for rapid shifts in time and location;
- juxtaposing past and present moments in the life of a character or characters.

Problem solving

During the intense work of refining story, scene, plot and character, problems will occur because of lack of dramatic structure. The following are some teaching strategies that could help overcome these types of difficulties.

Observing carefully the group's problems the teacher discusses how incorporation of metaphor and/or a symbol could help build their devised play into a cohesive whole. It would be important to remind students that a metaphor is a comparative device in playbuilding and it provides a new context and configuration for the dramatic meaning. A symbol is a mark, a sign, a thing that represents something in the drama; symbols in playbuilding help reinforce the overall meaning.

For example, if the sporting group were focusing on sailing they could set their drama in a metaphoric location such as the *The Good Ship Trustworthy* with the appropriate characters, and/or they could incorporate a sports object throughout the play as a symbol for honesty and integrity as well as dishonesty and intrigue. If this approach does not help to create a cohesive dramatic structure the teacher would ask each group to go back to the elements of drama and to pinpoint exactly how they are achieving each element and where the problems are. The groups bring these problems back to the class to see if collective thought can help solve the structural difficulties.

Phase four: performative phase (about one and half weeks)

All groups should use the assessment *of* learning task as a checklist to see if they have incorporated everything they wish to. Detailed rehearsals for character refinement might also be needed and this would include such things as:

- rehearsing the play without any dialogue;
- rehearsing the play with only subtext;
- speaking everything that is in the character's mind at a particular moment;
- justifying the character's actions at a given moment.

Each group should also costume and set their play in a realistic manner. It would be important to remind the students that the sets need only be a representation of location, and that all groups will have to act as stage hands to help get the different sets on or off stage as quickly as possible. There should be lighting and sound if appropriate.

At the end of the performance it would be beneficial for the students to explore the actor–audience relationship by asking their audience questions such as:

- Did you enjoy watching the performance style of realism? Why?
- Can you tell us what the elements of realism are from watching our plays?
- Were our characters fully realised and sustained throughout the play?
- Was our story and plot interesting and dramatically cohesive?

Within the following week students will hand in their written component and evaluate what they have learnt about the elements of drama and the performance style of realism while developing a single realistic character. This evaluation should include a discussion on how they might use this knowledge in other areas of their drama learning.

LOCATION-BASED PLAYBUILDING: MANIPULATING SETS IN ACTION

Unit description

In this unit of work students are given the opportunity to develop and design sets that allow the meaning of their play to be expressed, but not pre-empted by them. Once students start working from a set design their learning is extended and engaged so that they can effectively visualise their play within and because of the set. An important area to consider is that most schools do not have the capabilities to build elaborate and expensive sets for each playbuilding group's work, and therefore the sets the students design must be easily created and dismantled on the classroom floor using scenic elements. Location-based playbuilding does not always need an external audience as its focus is on work in progress which does not extend to the detailed playbuilding rehearsal phase as described in level 3 theme- and character-based playbuilding.

In this unit of work no formal assessment *of* learning task is given to the playbuilders. The threat of formal assessment activities in senior year can lead sometimes to despondency as it is not only the threat of formal assessment from the drama course, but the threat of formal assessment that arrives from every other course the students are undertaking. Therefore at the end of the unit of work there is an informal assessment *for* learning activity.

How long?

Suggested timeline is 5 weeks based on 4 × 50-minute lessons.

Phase one: generative phase (about two weeks)

The teacher explains to the class that they are going to make and create a group set design and explore how this impacts upon and helps develop their playbuilding ideas. There will be no formal assessment task in this unit of work as the focus of learning is on playbuilding in progress. There will be an assessment *for* learning activity at the end of this project, and this will be conducted through focus questions. No grading, marking or ranking will therefore be involved.

The class is then given starting points and dramatic timelines within which they will playbuild. Starting points to choose from:

- a landline telephone, modern or old-fashioned
- a mobile phone
- a letter.

You also have a choice of various imaginary timelines that will provide constraints on how you devise your plays:

- 10 minutes
- 1 hour
- 24 hours
- 1 week.

These imaginary timelines will help frame the dramatic action.

Questions that you should ask about the starting points and timelines are:

- What do these starting points have in common and what are the differences?
- Where could these starting points be located?
- How could the various imaginary timelines impact on the dramatic action?

The teacher reiterates these points by explaining:

Each of these starting points has embedded in its dramatic action characters outside the location. These characters may never be realised (seen) on stage but they could be an important part of the dramatic action. Each starting point has the possibility for a variety of locations where the dramatic action could be set, and added to this complexity is the impact of devising around an imaginary timeframe. Let's begin by taking the starting point of *A letter* and improvise with a chair to explore some of these possibilities.

The teacher places an armchair in the centre of the room and puts a book beside the chair. A letter is in the back of the book unknown to the student; it reads *Your life is in great danger*. The teacher asks one student to go to the chair and when they feel ready to sit down, pick up the book, and start reading. At an appropriate point the student is asked to turn to the back of the book, open the letter, read it, and react. This activity should take 20–40 seconds.

Questions are posed to the class and the student about this improvisation:

- What location did the armchair represent to you?
- Did the location take on a different mood when the student picked up the book and began to read? What and why?
- What impact did the letter have on the mood and location?

- What is the difference between a location and a set design and how was this demonstrated in the improvisation?

In this discussion the teacher introduces the idea that the location was a living room which has been created within a representational set design, where only one object, the armchair, was needed to give a suggestion of reality. The letter impacted on the location and the set design. A *set design* is different from a location as it can include a number of locations, *from a single unified set design vision*. The set design is there to help develop the storyline and plot and it is a dynamic place for the physical life of the actors.

This improvisation is carried out again with different types of chairs, such as a pew, a stool, an office chair. Similar questions are asked about how the location changed, and hence the characterisation and reaction to the letter, because of the different chairs used as a scenic element in the set design.

An extension improvisation is to place four similar chairs and a table in the centre of the classroom. On the table is a *mobile phone*. Four students are asked to be volunteers and are told that none of them is allowed to leave the location during the improvisation. The scenario is that they are four friends sharing a flat and none of them owns this mobile phone. The imaginary timeline for this improvisation is one hour. The students are given a role card and asked that they do not share it with the other students. These role cards have the following information:

- Student 1: you want to use the mobile phone without anyone noticing as you are going to try to make a deal to pick up a small amount of hashish.
- Student 2: you have just received a text message on that mobile phone saying that only you must use the phone, otherwise a friend's life could be in great danger.
- Student 3: you want to steal the mobile phone and take it to a party.
- Student 4: you want to phone your Mum and ask her over for the evening.

The group of students improvise this situation for 1–2 minutes and the class discusses:

- How did the mobile phone impact on the set design?
- How did the restriction of not leaving the location affect the dramatic action?
- Were there other characters that the audience did not see that impacted on the action?
- How did the imaginary timeline affect the dramatic action?
- What would change if this improvisation was set over 24 hours?

The teacher explains that when the playbuilding groups are formed each will create their own set design that will tell or help tell the story of their devised play. When they start this process they must remember that in the theatre the first visual image of the play is the set; from this the audience gain a wealth of information about characters, location, period and style. The set design should be a single dynamic image that captures the essence of their play.

Each group can create only one set with a unified scenic design. If the play they devise needs a couple of locations the set must not change; it will be through the acting that the set is endowed with a different location. Stage lighting can be part of their set design but blackouts are not allowed as this is a lazy solution to solving the problems of creating an imaginative and unified scenic design. *Furthermore groups will not actually build a set but they will use scenic elements to create sets.* If groups want to build a couple of scenic elements then of course they should be allowed to *but* the scenic elements the groups will in general use be already built and can be painted or rearranged to help create the dramatic effect they want.

Scenic elements

Scenic elements are, in the main, objects that are used to help transform an empty theatre stage into a set design. Scenic elements reflect the visual concept of a play, and are used to compose and transform the empty theatre space into an imaginative world for the play to inhabit. The classroom should have a variety of scenic elements that can help create the sets. There should be different types and styles of:

- blinds
- chairs
- cushions
- desks
- doors
- flats
- floor coverings
- lamps
- material
- roster boxes
- scenic paint
- scrims
- stools.

These types of scenic elements can be obtained from the school community or from scouring the local opportunity shops for interesting and unusual objects. Generally a drama department will not have enough scenic elements for each group's sole use; therefore the groups must learn to share the resources during the workshops.

Styles of sets

The class should explore different styles of set design that they might use in their work. The following handout would be given to the students to examine and discuss.

Set design
Your group's set design should engage the audience with sensory and visual information to support the ideas of your devised play. Your group will need to decide the style of the set design. You need to ask yourselves will it be staged:

- in a totally realistic manner?
- in a representational manner that lacks specific detail but suggests reality?
- in an abstract manner where the set is composed of different spaces and shapes?

- in an absurd manner that uses scenic elements to emphasise and overstate ideas?
- in a manner that combines different styles?

Whatever style your group decides upon, you must remember that the set design must convey a controlling message to the audience and sharply focus the ideas in your play.

When the class have finished discussing how the style of set design impacts on plays, the teacher creates an abstract set for them so that they can visualise one way to go about the task.

> **Handy hint . . .**
> *The class could refer to John Goodwin's textbook* British Theatre Design *(1989).*

Creating an abstract set

Three long pieces of material are hung from the drama workshop's lighting bars or ceiling. The teacher explains that these are going to be used to abstractly represent a hotel and what happens inside its walls.

> These three pieces of material can be used as the corridors of a hotel that a character(s) can walk or run through. They can represent different floors of the building.
> They can be used as doors to open, doors to hide behind and peep out of, and doors that lead into another room.
> They can also be used as a dress to try on for a ball at the hotel, as a partner to dance with, or as a champagne glass.
> Perhaps they momentarily can become a mobile phone, a letter, a table cloth that the maître d' is inspecting, or a baby a parent is holding, or a motor bike that someone is riding to get to the hotel.

As the teacher is explaining how the scenic elements of this abstract set work, she or he asks students to get up and demonstrate the different ways this material can be used to create a hotel and the action that happens inside it. This simultaneous action helps the students to visualise the capabilities of material to make dramatic meaning as an abstract set design.

Groupings

Using the talking circle is a way for students to discuss and know who is interested in what starting point and what timeline. From this knowledge the class forms interest groups of about 6–8 in a group. It is preferable that there are no more than 3–4 groups formed as this makes it easier to share the limited resources. The groups are given a couple of lessons to begin work on the task, with the teacher reminding them that the set must impact on their play but never override it unless that is intentional.

Phases two and three: constructing and structuring phases (about two weeks)

Because of the nature of this type of playbuilding, groups will be constructing and structuring simultaneously. It is important again to reiterate in this phase, as the groups are developing their playbuilding scenes from the starting points and imaginary timeline, that *the message of their play is to be enhanced by the location and the set design in action, not overridden by it.*

The elements of drama

In this phase an initial teaching strategy is for each group to work independently with the teacher to experiment how the elements of drama are impacting on their set design and hence the message in their devised play.

The teacher asks the groups to discuss or demonstrate the following dramatic moments:

- where the main focus of the set is;
- how this focus creates dramatic tension;
- what the characters' relationships are with (a) the location and (b) the set;
- how the set design helps create the mood of the play;
- how the scenic elements in the set design are used as symbols and how this impacts on the message in the play.

Solving problems

One of the main problems the playbuilders will encounter is how to articulate clearly what the controlling idea or vision is for their style of set. To help groups overcome this problem the teacher asks them to:

- Draw their set design in their workbooks and discuss how they see the unfolding storyline and plot being enacted in this environment. They need to be critical and discuss what problems and obstacles they encounter with this drawing and their visualisations. They should draw the set in relation to the type of stage they have chosen.
- The group should write up a set designer's concept. For example, the opening paragraph states the main story and/or plotline of their devised play, and the next paragraph discusses the overall concept that they as set designers are working with; this paragraph must include why they have taken this approach, the style of the set and type of stage they have chosen. The next paragraph could go into detail about how time and location, and the restrictions on these, have impacted on their set design. The closing paragraph must discuss the overall visual impact of the set and how it creates a message for their imaginary audience.

Types of stages

The teacher gives the individual groups a worksheet describing the different types of stage spaces that they can create their devising within (see Figure 6.3). Experienced playbuilders will most probably have already thought about this, but it is always good to revise their previous drama learning, and to remind them that their style of set can be fitted onto a type of stage; they can achieve this in the classroom by using masking tape on the floor to indicate the circumference of their stage and where they imagine the audience would be.

PROSCENIUM STAGES

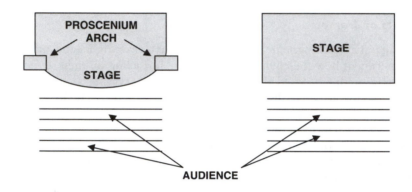

THRUST STAGES

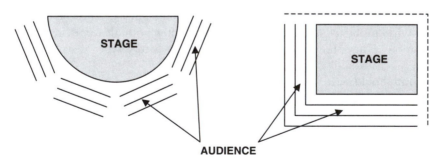

Figure 6.3 Types of stages

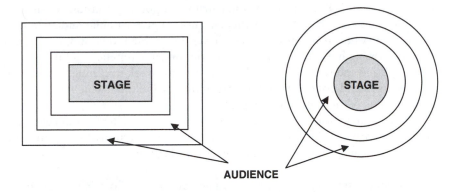

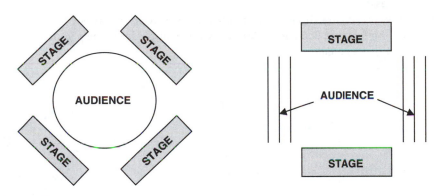

Figure 6.3 continued

Set as a linking device

The groups should be encouraged to use the set, and the scenic elements within it, to create their linkings. For example, if they are using material as an abstract set design, one scene could link to another by the imaginative use of the material to create the transitions, or if they were using a representational set made up of chairs, the chairs could be used to create the dramatic shape from one moment to the next, or the groups could use any tangible or imagined scenic element to merge one moment in time with another.

Phase four: performative phase (about one week)

In this last week the groups should be given individual time in the classroom with the scenic elements they require. The whole class should make up a rehearsal roster so that they all participate in a collaborative manner in this important decision making. They should also be reminded that although they are not having a public audience for this playbuilding, their work in progress will be viewed by each another and, if appropriate, another drama class with the same experience or on the same timetabling line.

Costume, lighting and sound should all be part of this week's refining, but these production elements should not override the focus of the playbuilding, which is on set design that allows meaning of their play to be expressed.

After the class have performed their work in progress the teacher introduces an assessment *for* learning activity. This is done by creating focus questions for the students to answer in discussion and as a written reflection and evaluation:

- How did the starting point and timeframe your group chose impact on your set design?
- How did your group go about choosing and creating a style and type of set?
- How did your group solve the problems associated with creating a set design with limited resources?
- How did your set help create your story?
- What have you learnt about creating stories in location playbuilding during this process?
- How can you use this learning in other areas of your education?
- Did the fact that you had no formal assessment hinder or help your work, or did it make no difference?

Part III

Playbuilding for all

Learning from theatre practitioners

Teaching considerations

This chapter involves the exploration of two theatre practitioners and how their theatrical philosophies, techniques and practices can be integrated into a playbuilding unit of work. We have chosen Ariane Mnouchkine and Bertolt Brecht as the theatre practitioners as their conventions, techniques and performance styles are distinctive, giving rise to two very different and divergent playbuilding projects. Furthermore, their theatrical practices utilise and value metaphoric transformation and the individual's imagination to generate collective creativity. These are two very important aspects of playbuilding that need continual nurturing in a drama learning environment.

The concept behind integrating theatre practitioners into playbuilding is to allow the students an opportunity for creative fusion. This ensures that the students do not mimic the ideas and practices of theatre practitioners, but that they manipulate, expand and learn from them to tell their own stories and to make their own dramatic meaning. When planning a unit of work it is important for the teacher to choose what they think are the fundamental learning areas for their students and, if appropriate, or time permits, to add more. Incorporated into this type of playbuilding are teaching strategies that provide openings for playbuilders to apply their embodied learning into their written work.

Learner profile

Students who undertake this type of playbuilding will be intermediate or experienced playbuilders and will be willing to explore and research theatre practitioners' conventions, techniques, and performance styles, and then to apply this learning to their own project.

ARIANE MNOUCHKINE: FORMING A STUDENT THEATRE COMPANY

Unit description

In this unit of work students learn about Ariane Mnouchkine's Théâtre du Soleil's highly theatrical collaborative processes and devising practices which they integrate into their own playbuilding project when they form a student theatre company. The starting point for their playbuilding emerges from this theatre practitioner's philosophy and the playbuilders select and manipulate her theatrical practices to make meaning for them; this means that the impulse for their playbuilding will come from a *topic*. The student theatre company performs their devised play in front of an external audience and the company is required to write a response to the process and performances.

How long?

Suggested time is 10 weeks based on 4 × 50-minute lessons per week. It is also important to provide the students with a weekend rehearsal so that they simulate Théâtre du Soleil workshop and rehearsal conditions.

Phase one: generative phase (about one week)

Groupings

Similar to Ariane Mnouchkine's politics of creative collaboration, the class will work as an ensemble throughout the entire process.

Initial teaching strategies

The students will need to do some preparation for the project, which would take a few days to complete. The following worksheet is handed out and read through with the teacher.

> Student Theatre Company Meeting
> Imagine that you are a group of student actors who have formed a Student Theatre Company. This company's aim is to excel in devising theatre around issues of contemporary history, such as immigration or youth employment. The performance style of your Student Theatre Company will be overtly theatrical as the company believes exaggerated and heightened acting styles engage and entertain an audience.

The company is holding a meeting where each actor will discuss the skills and ideas they have brought to past devised performances and what they can bring to this newly formed Student Theatre Company. This meeting will be run by the Stage Manager.

When the class has read the worksheet the teacher explains that each student will create a role as a student actor. They need to give themselves a fictitious name, age, and style of performance that they excel in such as Melodrama, Physical Theatre, Cabaret, *Commedia dell' Arte*. The role play of the Student Theatre Company meeting will be explored in class with the teacher as the Stage Manager.

> **Handy hint . . .**
> *Build on students' past knowledge of performance styles in this project.*

The teacher in role as the Stage Manager welcomes all the students in role as the actors of this new Student Theatre Company. The Stage Manager introduces him- or herself and discusses the advantages of a Student Theatre Company that devises its own work about contemporary history in an overtly theatrical manner. The Stage Manager then asks each actor, in turn, to say why they believe this Student Theatre Company is needed, and to discuss or demonstrate their appropriate performance skills. At the end of this role play the teacher and students step out of role and discuss the improvisation, with the teacher connecting its structure to Ariane Mnouchkine and Théâtre du Soleil.

The playbuilders will need to know background information, which can be handed out as a worksheet, such as:

- Ariane Mnouchkine has been called the most significant French theatre director of the twentieth and twenty-first centuries because of her brilliance in devising engaging and relevant theatre for a global world.
- She is the founder of Théâtre du Soleil which began in 1959 (although under another name) and is still thriving today.
- She sees theatre as a collaborative effort that is a service to the community.
- Her devised plays, with Théâtre du Soleil, are based on history as she believes that history impacts on the individual and the community, and that it can be used to confront and entertain audiences about the struggles of the twenty-first century.
- Her plays are highly stylised events which use a kaleidoscope of sound, music, sumptuous costumes and hyperbolic characters.
- She believes that theatre above all must be theatrical.
- Her theatre explores and reinterprets highly stylised theatre forms such as Melodrama, Romantic Theatre, Cabaret, *Commedia dell'Arte*, Kathakali, Noh Drama, Kabuki Theatre, and Balinese Dance/Drama.
- Her approach is to sharpen the senses of her ensemble and audience by mixing and reinterpreting such forms.
- Her teaching methods advocate the visual and non-verbal aspects of theatre.
- She uses improvisation and transformation techniques to develop her storyline.
- Her storylines are often structured as a parable that illustrates a moral lesson.
- Costumes, character, mask and chorus underpin her principles of exploring a topic.
- She stages her plays in non-traditional theatre structures, such as gymnasiums and her audience literally go on a journey with the actors, although there are usually areas for the audience to be seated.

The students should continue with individual and group research throughout the project.

> **Handy hint . . .**
> *Students could refer to J. Miller's textbook in the Routledge Performance Practitioners series* Ariane Mnouchkine *(2007) or D. Williams' textbook* Collaborative Theatre *(1999).*

After the playbuilders have discussed and debated this practitioner's ways of devising theatre, the teacher explains that they are going to blend her philosophies, conventions, techniques and performance styles into their playbuilding project. They will be starting with her principles of embarking on a journey together that encourage community collaboration. It is important for students to record these principles in their workbooks.

- Each student is asked to acknowledge everyone in the classroom at the beginning of every rehearsal. This means that no one is too busy to greet or be greeted.
- Everyone must listen to each other and learn from their points of view during the process and final performances.
- All students will help with all aspects of the playbuilding – which means they are all the playwrights, directors, actors, musicians, designers, stage hands, promotion personnel as well as the cleaners of the space.

Teaching strategies to develop these principles

Continuous hand holding

The aim of the activity is always to have both hands connected with someone else. To begin, everyone must be holding one person's hand to shake and one person's hand to be connected with. The students introduce themselves to the person they are shaking hands with while never letting go of the other hand of a student that they are not verbally engaging with. Using this process the whole class tries to shake hands with everyone in the group within two minutes. An extension to this exercise is that, as they shake hands, students explore vocal dynamics through pitch, pace and tone or tell each other about topics that interest them for playbuilding around.

Rhythmic naming

The aim of the activity is to explore rhythm, voice, movement and simple chorus techniques. All the students stand in a circle and set up a simple rhythm (e.g. stamp stamp, clap clap, vocal sound vocal sound). Once the rhythm has been established one student starts by saying their own name and the whole group repeats it. This process is repeated by the next student and so on. Once the students have started to develop their characters they would explore this activity in role.

Musical rhythms

The aim of the activity is to explore music as a source of inspiration. A piece of rhythmic music is used that is unfamiliar to the students, such as Erik Satie or Beethoven's lesser-known works. The students move around the room using the musical rhythms and working against the musical rhythms. The teacher explains that they have become musical magnets and when she or he signals (by holding an arm in the air) the students are drawn, in rhythm, to the person nearest them so that their bodies are touching, and when her or his arm is lowered they split apart. An extension to this activity is that when students have developed their characters they find music that suits their character's personality and download it onto an ipod. This individual music can be used in warm-up activities that help the students to develop their character's internal and external rhythms.

After each of these activities it is important to explain to the students how they connect to the theatrical principles in Ariane Mnouchkine's Théâtre du Soleil. For example,

Continuous hand holding is to demonstrate that there is a continuous community connection between every student. *Rhythmic naming* is to develop an awareness of different rhythms; control of delivery and response to other actors' cues and *Musical rhythms* is to explore music as a source of inspiration as well as to develop the musicality of the actor and their developing character.

> **Handy hint . . .**
> *These types of teaching strategies, which relate directly to the practitioner's philosophies, can be revised throughout the whole unit of work.*

Phase two: constructing phase (about two weeks)

Costumed characters, chorus and masks

Once the playbuilders have grasped how to embark on a collaborative journey together, they are introduced to Ariane Mnouchkine's initial improvisation practices that explore the potential of costumed characters, chorus and masks. These improvisations are designed to develop students' spontaneity and intuition.

Developing a costumed character

The classroom should be scattered with flamboyant costumes and rich coloured material. When the students enter they are allowed the freedom to try on, and mix and match, as many types of costumes as they wish. At an appropriate time the teacher stops their students' exploration and discusses how they have felt about this free association with character and costume. A suggested discussion could be:

> In your improvisations you have freely experimented with how costume can create the shape and texture of a character. How does this feel? What have you discovered? Ariane Mnouchkine and her actors from Théâtre du Soleil begin their devising processes in this same way, and just like them you are now going to extend this activity by exploring the internal and external moods of your developing costumed character.

The costumed playbuilders are asked to work in pairs to create an exaggerated sculpture of the following emotions:

- love, hate, fright, surprise.

An extension of this activity is to give the pairs of students contrasting emotions:

- joy/grieving, trust/suspicion, cheerfulness/melancholy.

The students discuss the key theatrical findings from their improvisation, such as how a costumed character's physical actions and internal emotions are linked together, or how costume and stylised movements can enhance or detract from the dramatic meaning.

Further discussion about costumed characters could be:

> Ariane Mnouchkine believes that theatre work begins with searching for characters from costumes. She believes there is no subtext in this exploration as the skin of an actor is the costume, and costume helps establish characters. As your process of devising progresses, your characters will change or others will emerge that help generate ideas for your show. This will happen as you continually explore different ways to costume yourselves.

Costumed chorus work

From these types of discussions the improvisations should seamlessly extend into costumed chorus work with the teacher initially explaining:

> Ariane Mnouchkine also believes that costumed characters should become a chorus at vital moments in the play and that a chorus can introduce the theatrical element of spectacle. Costumed chorus exploration is therefore pivotal to bringing dramatic action to life and it can heighten emotions in scenes.

Using the same concept of exploring the costumed character through emotion, break the class into two and ask both groups to become a chorus that responds in stylised rhythmic unison, but with different physical reactions, to the same emotions. The separate groups show each other their work and discuss why Ariane Mnouchkine believes chorus is a vital key to bringing dramatic action to life, and whether any of their costumed improvisations touched on the elements of spectacle.

Costumed mask work

The last teaching strategy in phase two is to introduce students to the importance of costumed mask work. Students most probably will have worked with masks before but it is always important to go back to the basics when re-exploring the creative power of masks. Depending on the resources of the school, the playbuilders can use such masks as *Commedia dell'Arte*, theatrical make-up, white powder or even scarves. In costume the students don a mask; to begin with, they slowly, and with great interest:

- inspect themselves completely from all angles;
- explore their gestures and movements;
- observe what other characters are doing but do not approach them;
- extend their inspecting to look at the room they are in;
- examine and explore all the windows and their functions;
- examine and explore all the chairs and their functions;
- go in and out of the doors;
- find a place in the room where they make themselves at home (adapted from Appel 1982).

When this exploration is finished the students discuss their observations and why they think mask work is an integral factor to this type of playbuilding. The teacher needs to introduce the principles of masks and the following discussion could take place.

> Ariane Mnouchkine believes that costumed masked characters help build a meta-phoric story as they can allow the audience to see truths about lives and situations that are sometimes hidden. She believes that actors must develop the masks, through improvisation, into modern characters that are relevant to the topics in her plays. She asks her actors to give life to the mask and invent emotional and physical details for it. As playbuilders you will start developing these principles throughout your process.

> *Handy hint . . .*
>
> *In each workshop for costumed character, chorus and mask remind the students of the importance of creating highly stylised and theatrical improvisations.*

At some point, while these three principles of costumed character, chorus and mask are being explored, the students discuss why history is an important area to devise collaborative theatre around. The teacher could explain that Ariane Mnouchkine's theatre explores history in an attempt to understand its impact on society. She wants to encourage her audience to be part of the historical process and to see themselves as part of a system that can be changed or acted upon. In her work with Théâtre du Soleil she sees history as more than past events, but as a living story that connects to contemporary societies. The key question the students have to ask themselves is what does history mean to them and what can they, as a whole class, playbuild around, using history as a source of inspiration. The playbuilders are asked to think about areas of history that interest them and to start collecting past and present historical information from books, newspapers, television, the internet, blog sites.

Group writing

As the students explore costumed characters, chorus and masks they will write about their improvisations; this means that they will be recording and reflecting on their workshop experiences so that at the end of the project they can, as a Student Theatre Company, publish their work. During this process they will write from a group's perspectives as well as from their own.

At reflective moments after these improvisations the teacher will ask the students to form three or four groups. The groups should be made up of mixed-ability writers with students alternating as the scribes. Each group is asked to respond, in writing, to the improvisations and they can be given models of how to do this. The following models give the groups a topic sentence to lead into their responses, but many groups will rearrange the models to make their own response:

- We found it great fun to explore a character from the costumes scattered around the classroom floor. We found it challenging that . . .

- When our Student Theatre Company improvised the costumed chorus scene we all became characters that . . .
- When we experimented with the masks we found the atmosphere in the classroom was very intense. This is similar to what Ariane Mnouchkine wants when she asks her actors to improvise with masks. We . . .

During this writing students can also record their own personal responses:

- When I became a chorus member I tried to exaggerate my acting style so as to affect the audience as Ariane Mnouchkine's ensemble would. I . . .

When the writing is complete the groups share it with one another. It is important to point out to the class that this writing is just the beginning of a rough theatrical draft, and the way the group expresses their experiences is important but they will improve with practice. These types of writing strategies can be used throughout the whole playbuilding project. These group writing moments can be assessment *for* learning activities as the teacher can gauge from the responses how the playbuilders are responding to the process.

Phase three: structuring phase (about four weeks)

Groupings

The class works as an ensemble.

Assessment of learning task

An assessment *of* learning task should be given at the beginning of phase three as students are about to embark on applying their developing skills, knowledge and understanding to a whole-class playbuilding project. This assessment *of* learning task could be prepared during the teacher's planning of the unit, or it could be developed during phase two when the teacher understands what interests the students, and what type of assessment task would be appropriate.

The assessment *of* learning task given here empowers the students, *as an ensemble*, to come up with the answers to the task rather than giving them criteria to work from, but of course a teacher could make up detailed criteria if required. When the teacher hands out this task she or he explains that the whole class are going to create a Student Theatre Company that will playbuild in the style of Ariane Mnouchkine's Théâtre du Soleil.

Assessment *of* learning task

- Your class will form a Student Theatre Company that will devise a 30–45-minute performance in the style of Ariane Mnouchkine's Théâtre du Soleil.
- Your Company believes that theatre is a service to the community and are going to devise a play that connects what has happened in history to what is happening today.
- Your play is going to be overtly theatrical.
- Your play will take place in five weeks' time; location to be decided.

- Your Student Theatre Company will write a reflective response to your process and performance to be published within your community.

The following questions will help your Company with all aspects of the production. Why does Ariane Mnouchkine believe in:

- devised collaborative theatre?
- exploring history as a topic to devise around?
- the importance of the actor's vocal and physical domains?
- exploring costumes as the second skin of the actor?
- chorus work as a dynamic way to help tell the story?
- the language of masks?
- music and sound as an integral part of the dramatic colouring?
- using the form of a parable to tell the story?
- using a non-traditional theatre space?
- a fluid actor–audience relationship?
- the importance of a highly stylised theatre?

Choosing a topic

When the class have read the assessment task and asked questions to clarify points, they should spend a lesson revising the importance of using history as a metaphor to playbuild around. They could discuss Théâtre du Soleil plays such as *1798*, which explores the French Revolution but directly connects with periods of adversity in modern-day France, or *L'Age d'Or*, which investigates everyday struggles with a particular focus on immigration; the class may eventually come up with topics such as:

- history of children in the industrial revolution
- youth employment
- children of cyberspace
- immigration.

Once the topic has been chosen the development process begins. In this hypothetical situation we have chosen *not to choose a topic* but given specific teaching strategies that can be applied to any topic playbuilders choose.

Performance style and parable

It is important early on in phase three to decide on an overtly theatrical performance style that the playbuilders have preferably learnt before. For example, if the class has already learnt about Cabaret, *Commedia dell' Arte*, Melodrama or Noh Theatre they could discuss whether any of these styles would be suitable, or whether it would be better to merge these styles using contemporary characters and situations.

Once the performance style or styles is/are chosen and revised, the playbuilders could use the structure of a parable for their topic. The parable structure is sometimes used by Ariane Mnouchkine to give an *engaging lesson* to the audience in a theatrical manner; a parable also has metaphoric devising properties. Students could individually research the structure or the teacher could give them a simple parable structure to begin the research process.

> A simple parable structure:
> - A parable has a simple storyline.
> - It sketches out a setting, but this setting can change.
> - It creates dramatic action through characters facing moral dilemmas and making questionable decisions and having to live by the consequences.
> - The characters change in some way. For some, the change is of new insights, for others the change may be new relationships or the change could be from life to death.
> - The parable can be a metaphor for history and it will have a symbolic message about a realistic situation in life.

Through the parable structure the Student Theatre Company can explore the chosen performance style, the developing storyline and the characters in the story. The parable could emerge from newspaper or internet stories or any other type of research. The Company improvises the different stories and discusses what possibilities they have, remembering they want a simple but consistent dramatic through line. When the parable begins to emerge, some useful character teaching strategies could be explored using the information in the research material:

- Students discover their character's stance, gesture, walk, prop, independent activity and vocal dynamics.
- Students explore their character's everyday life, like waiting for a bus or reading a book, to more complex situations of getting into trouble, or moments of great indignity or frustration.
- Students explore their character's playfulness and stubbornness in the given situation with other characters.
- A CD is created containing sounds that relate directly to a location in the play. The students are asked to listen to this and to think of it as a musical score. From this musical score they build a situation in which their characters live and/or work in, encounter one another, have arguments and conflict, and try to keep conflicts hidden (adapted from Lemasson 1999).

From all these types of improvisation there is a discussion about what the characters have in common and/or what the differences are in relation to the research material and the developing scenes. Using the findings from these discussions the class explores how their characters, as a chorus, can create a dramatic impact on the parable. They explore:

- standing and sitting together while reacting to the research;
- ritualised movements that respond to the research;
- physically and vocally reacting to events that have occurred prior to the action of the research;
- physically and vocally interrupting and/or commenting on the conflict between characters or poking fun at situations.

At the end of every class the company discuss the outcomes from these improvisations and how they could elaborate on them to create pertinent scenes. When scenes are created the company links them together to create a theatrical fluidity. They could explore such linkings as:

- spotlights to follow the action as it changes;
- microphones or loudspeakers to change the action;
- using the part mobile audience to create a new dramatic meaning;
- using musical instruments to introduce a shift in the action;
- using the chorus to evoke dramatic change.

Group writing while making the play

A number of times during this phase it is important for students to continue with reflective writing in their designated writing groups.

The groups continue with similar writing strategies as introduced in phase two, or if the teacher wishes, these could be extended. For example, groups could critique Ariane Mnouchkine's theatrical practices by creating a list of questions that they wish to ask her, or use the questions from their assessment handout. The drama technique they would use for the practitioner questioning is *Hot Seating*. It is important to remind students that anyone in the group can become Ariane Mnouchkine at a time decided upon by the group, so there can be a lot of Arianes in this activity who will respond to many questions. During this process the verbal responses can be jotted down by group members or they can record what was said and transcribe it back. An extension of this activity would be to hot seat members of their Student Theatre Company and ask them questions about their processes.

Another useful group writing strategy is for each student to simultaneously say and write what has meant a lot to them during this developmental process. This could be followed by individual problems that they have encountered, and how they have tried to solve them, and finished by the group writing one phrase that attempts to convey their feeling about the playbuilding project. These activities are great fun and can create headings and structures for the final writing.

Organising the writing into headings

The last group writing activity is to help the class to organise their reflective writings and to create an initial *order of importance* for their written work. This could be from central ideas they have discovered, to less central, or it could a linear timeline of the process their Student Theatre Company has undergone, or they could make headings to compare and contrast their work discussing all the positive aspects and then the negative aspects of the project. This organising task would be at the very end of phase three to help students put their thinking and writing in order. The writing groups will not go back to their written reflective work until after the play is over.

Phase four: performative phase (about three weeks)

The space where the play will be performed, such as a school auditorium or a gymnasium, may need to be decided at the very beginning of the unit due to school logistics. Generally students will not have access to this space until a couple of weeks before the performance but as soon as they do the Student Theatre Company need to decide how they wish to establish the acting area, and the type of relationship they want with their audience. The teacher could discuss with the students that:

> Ariane Mnouchkine believes in the concept of an empty space in which to create collaborative theatre and she generally uses community spaces such as a gymnasium or a factory. These unconventional theatre spaces allow her the opportunity to create a dynamic that is new and challenging for the actors and the audience. For example, as the audience arrives, the actors are often visible, preparing their make-up and costumes and her theatre programmes can provide a collage of historical documentation that relates directly to the play. Within the play itself the audience can be mobile if they wish or in designated seating areas; sometimes they can become part of a scene or interject if appropriate to the style and content of the play. These are the type of decisions your company must now make.

Once these decisions have been made intensive rehearsals begin. It is important to remind the Student Theatre Company that every rehearsal must start with each company member acknowledging each other, and to use the talking circle to find out everybody's view of problems and how to solve and manage them, and it is also important for the teacher to have a rehearsal checklist to act upon. For example:

* Does the play's performance style need to be theatrically heightened?
* Are the characters fully developed and sustained physically and vocally?
* Do the chorus scenes create a dramatic effectiveness in helping to tell the story?
* Do the costumes and masks present a unified concept of the play?
* Are the costumes elaborate and rich in texture and colour and do they effectively communicate the characters' purpose and function in the play?
* Does the parable have a sophisticated structure and a dramatic coherence?
* Do the scenic requirements help realise the play's message?

Any of the teaching strategies already discussed in levels 1, 2 or 3 would be useful to refine these dramatic points.

The Student Theatre Company would also need to decide what information and visual design concept would go onto the promotion and programme material. The teacher should encourage the students to use their research material while creating a poster and programme, and that the design concept needs to relate directly to the play they have created.

The play should be performed a number of times so that the students can immerse themselves in the workings of their Student Theatre Company. The performances should be video-recorded as a testament to their achievements.

Verbal and written reflections

After the performances the Student Theatre Company should watch the videos, discuss and write down their collective responses to these final experiences.

They would then create a Student Theatre Company newspaper. For example, each group could break down their written responses created throughout the project into sections and then into articles, interviews, letters, and/or reviews; different groups could be responsible for different sections. This approach would also give the students the opportunity to publish photographs of the process and performance and to manipulate their promotions and programme material into an article. The students could publish their newspaper for the school community, or create a blog site for it, and even send it with video clips to Ariane Mnouchkine at Théâtre du Soleil.

BERTOLT BRECHT: PLAYBUILDING AN ESSAY

Unit description

In this unit of work students learn about and playbuild around Bertolt Brecht's political and artistic goals in conjunction with the thematic concerns of his play *Mother Courage and Her Children*. This means that they are playbuilding around a much larger starting point than is usually the case. An essay-style question for the playbuilding emerges from this theatre practitioner's practices, and will be answered through performance and also by an individual written drama essay. The project is performed in front of an external audience and is called *Playbuilding an Essay*.

How long?

Suggested timeline is 8 weeks based on 4 × 50-minute lessons a week.

Conceptual information for the teacher

The factual information on Bertolt Brecht and *Mother Courage and Her Children* in this unit of work, given via worksheets, is aimed to provide students with a brief overview; therefore the playbuilders will need to do extra research throughout the process. It is also important to remind students that this is not a theoretical study of Bertolt Brecht and his play *but a playbuilding unit* where they use Brecht's theatrical practices to make their own play.

Also the concept behind playbuilding an essay (also known as performing an essay; see Lovesy 2002, 2003, 2005b) is that many drama students struggle to write drama essays because of their predominant kinaesthetic learning styles (Gardner 1993), and through specific teaching strategies students can be given the opportunity to:

- Create a playbuilt essay on the stage floor. Teaching strategies initially include a variety of whole-class improvisation activities that illuminate a theatre practitioner's practices. From these whole-class experimentations smaller playbuilding groups are formed, and the participating groups are given an essay question to answer through performance so as to affect their audience as if they were the readers of a senior drama written essay. So just as in an essay, points or aspects of argument need to be made and backed up by evidence, all this should be acted out in the form of playbuilding.

- Transfer this embodied learning to their individual drama written essays.

Phase one: generative phase (about one week)

Groupings

In phase one students are taught as a whole class, as well as being taught in smaller groups.

Group writing

After each activity groups of students are asked to write about their experiences. This group writing is free form; there is no right or wrong way for the group to approach it. The group shares their work with the rest of the class members and the written work is placed around the classroom to be analysed and reflected upon by all.

Play reading, research and improvisations

Throughout the introductory phase it is important to explain to the students that eventually they will be playbuilding in response to an essay question about the fusion between their playbuilding ideas and the practitioner's theatrical practices; this will be answered through performance and as an individual written essay.

At the beginning of this phase the class are given a copy of the play *Mother Courage and Her Children*.

> **Handy hint . . .**
> At the time of writing we recommend the 1996 Arcade Paperback edition that has been adapted by David Hare.

Students actively read this play in class and for homework, focusing on its thematic concerns and dramatic action. Students are also given an overview of the play *Mother Courage and Her Children* and its thematic concerns. They are asked to come to class with questions about this worksheet.

- Bertolt Brecht wrote *Mother Courage and Her Children* at the beginning of World War II in response to the devastation that he foresaw.
- Brecht's play is about the futility of war.
- The main character is Mother Courage. Mother Courage is shrewd, cynical, and quick-witted but she is oblivious to her own decline throughout the play.
- Brecht said that, as a character, Mother Courage learns nothing, absolutely nothing during the course of the play. War in fact is Mother Courage's deadly partner. She is not a heroine, she is a flawed woman. She is a woman of opposites – she loves and she hates, she uses people and she cares for people; ultimately she is a woman out for herself.

- The play opens when she is separated from one of her children and by the end of the play she loses all three children because of her mercenary nature.
- Throughout the play she hopes to profit by the war without being harmed by it; she runs a canteen wagon that follows the army around and sells items to the soldiers.
- At the end of the play she also loses her livelihood as a trader of wares.
- This is also a business play because it suggests that war is the continuation of business by almost any means.

The teacher asks the students what questions they have about this worksheet overview but also needs to make sure that pivotal areas are covered such as:

- What are the themes that have emerged from this overview?
- Why would a playwright write a play about these themes?
- Why do you think the main character is called Mother Courage?
- Where and what are the power dynamics in this outline?

Two small groups are asked to create a simple image of the themes and overview of the play. One group does this symbolically and the other realistically. The teacher facilitates the building of the images by asking such questions as:

- What is the first image of power?
- Who are the perpetrators of this power?
- Who are the victims?
- Where is there an image of powerlessness?
- Where would be the playwright in this image?

The students who remain in the class as audience members are asked to sketch or note their responses to the two different images. The purpose of these images and the responses is to introduce the class to the concept that epic theatre uses the simplest possible groupings to express an overall sense of the issues at hand, and this is done both symbolically and realistically.

Students should also be given an overview of Brecht as the next improvisation will build upon their growing knowledge and understanding.

- The German playwright Bertolt Brecht was born in 1898 and died in 1956.
- Brecht's philosophy behind his plays was that he wanted his audience, whom he called spectators, to think deeply about the political issues. (A spectator is a person who observes, thinks and reflects on the dramatic action, rather than one who has been encouraged to surrender to the cathartic purging of the emotions.)
- Brecht's theatre is called epic theatre. Epic theatre is about changing the perspective from which a play is watched. Brecht's focus is on a theatre that 'appeals less to the feelings than to the spectator's reason' (Willett 1964, p. 23).
- To achieve epic theatre Brecht created and used many theatrical techniques such as:

  ○ Alienation, chorus, dialectics and argument, gestus, historification, montage, narrators, use of signs and words projected onto a screen, use of music and song, set designs that destroy illusions and generalised characters (in his plays actors played multiple roles that represent and demonstrate generalised characters).

- An underlying principle of epic theatre is one thing occurring after another in discrete steps.

The teacher discusses the key issues in the initial information, and reiterates that Brecht's epic theatre, his artistic and political goals, the different ways he sought to bring large and complex events onto the stage will all be considered in this playbuilding project, and that the epic theatre techniques outlined will become clearer to them as the unit of work progresses.

> *Handy hint . . .*
> *In this playbuilding project it is important that the students explore Brecht's theatre practices not as fixed or unchangeable, but as practices that can be elaborated upon or simplified to help them make meaning in their own work.*

To understand these key issues groups of 5–6 create an image of one aspect of this initial information that appeals to them. They can sketch signs or create banners and incorporate these into the image. The dramatised image is brought to life for 30 seconds using movement, dialogue and the signs.

The groups should interpret this improvisation in their own way and when the image has been completed the teacher takes photographs with a number of the students' mobiles and projects them onto a screen. These photographs are initially used to provoke discussion about what the class have included and why, what they don't understand and why, and how this type of improvisation and the photographs could be used in their forthcoming playbuilding project.

Phase two: constructing phase (about one week)

Exploring dialectics in the character of Mother Courage

From the students' growing understanding about the play and Brecht's theatre practices, an improvisation is introduced to explain dialectics to the playbuilders.

- All students mill around the room and the teacher explains that in different-sized groups they are going to demonstrate the contradictions in Mother Courage's personality.
- In pairs they then create an image of Mother Courage as fearless, then as fickle. In fours they create an image of Mother Courage as maternal and caring, then as emotionally aloof. In sixes they create an image of war as the great provider for Mother Courage, then war as the greater destroyer of her.

This is followed by discussion about the function of dialectics. For example:

> You have just been exploring the contradictions, the opposition of forces, in Mother Courage's character; this is called dialectics. Dialectics have the capacity to negate the spectators' concepts of the world, which are taken for granted. To be a spectator of a Brechtian play is to be forced to take decisions, because of the oppositions put forward. Which improvisations did you see, or were in, that made you think about the different aspects of dialectics and why did this happen?
>
> It is also very important to remember in your forthcoming playbuilding to incorporate dialectics however you see fit.

Analysis and improvisation of scene one

The aim of this improvisation is to introduce students to the importance of alienation, montage, song and signs in epic theatre. Students actively read scene one and create a written analysis of it. The following example is the type of key issues the students should be encouraged to find.

Plotline of scene one

- Scene one is set in Sweden in 1624. It is the beginning of the Thirty Years' War. The opening of scene one is where a Sergeant and Recruiting Officer are recruiting soldiers. The Officer is complaining of the difficulty of recruiting trustworthy soldiers, while the Sergeant declares that the people could use a good war as without war there is no organisation in society. A harmonica or Jewish harp is heard and a wagon appears on stage in which sits Mother Courage and her mute daughter Kattrin. The wagon is pulled by her two sons. Mother Courage sings a song trying to entice the soldiers to buy her wares.

Analysis of themes in scene one

- The entire play is foreshadowed in this opening scene. Mother Courage predicts doom for her family during her pantomime of fortune telling. Her attempts to sell things by predicting her customers' deaths only end up in predicting her own childrens' deaths. Even the manner of their deaths is provided: Eilif will die in war, Swiss Cheese due to his honesty, and Kattrin by not remaining mute. Mother Courage's song, *come and buy* is quickly transformed into the ironic *come and die*. This is Brecht's parody. The song's brilliance lies in its accuracy; you are a soldier if you are Mother Courage's customer and consequently you will likely be sent to your death. Buying from Mother Courage is almost symbolic, a foreshadowing of your own pending doom. She is therefore calling the men not only to buy, but also to die. Historification is present in this first scene as Brecht was re-examining the history of the Thirty Years' War by emphasising specific confronting events in the hope that his play would be heard and listened to by the people of 1939 Europe.

Once the class have completed this analysis they are asked, in groups of 4–6, to create an improvisation.

Using the analysis as skeleton background, create an improvisation where Mother Courage's song *come and buy* foreshadows the soldiers' pending doom. You must use some dialogue from the song and remember that your melody will be discordant in accordance with epic theatre principles. Some members of your group will create a silent language to indicate the parody and subtext of the song, which is *come and die*. You can use banners, signs, mobile phones, ipods, props, to enhance your improvisation as well as alienation and montage techniques. Remember that alienation can be thought of as halting the flow of the dramatic action to make the spectator look again, and montage can be thought of as juxtaposing moments against each other to create dramatic meaning which would shock spectators.

The groups rehearse and perform their improvisations. They discuss how they tried to achieve the task. The class should analyse and improvise other scenes from the play as well as acting them out as per the playscript.

Improvisation into Brecht's political goals

This final improvisation is to encourage students to think about Brecht's political goals.

- Students are grouped into the generalised characters from the play. Some become the Soldiers and the Commander-in Chief, others Mother Courage, others Mother Courage's children, others The Peasants, The Cook, The Chaplin, and some Bertolt Brecht. They are asked to find lines of dialogue from the play, or associated research, that indicates their political and/or social position on the purpose and function of a war. This dialogue and/or research must be used in the improvisation but it can be altered, added to, or elaborated upon. All students, in role, mill around the room. There is a chair in the centre of the classroom. When a character takes control of the chair they didactically barrage all others about their character's view of the Thirty Years' War. The other generalised characters become hecklers for and against this proposition.
- This activity can be elaborated upon by asking students to research reasons why governments go to war or not. From this research the students become the common people of the twentieth and twenty-first centuries. When a student takes control of the chair they become a didactic political activist and they barrage the common people with the benefits for or against war. The common people become hecklers for and against this proposition.

Students discuss and debate their own and Brecht's political goals. This improvisation could be used as an assessment *for* learning activity as it demonstrates to the teacher where students need help in developing their understanding of this theatre practitioner's philosophies.

> **Handy hint . . .**
> *Don't forget that the groups should be writing down their active explorations and sharing these with the rest of the class.*

At the end of this phase it is important to reiterate the purpose and function of these improvisations to the students.

> The improvisations we have been exploring over the last weeks are the building blocks to help you to create a playbuilt essay on the stage floor. You can think of these improvisations as draft paragraph scenes that you might use in your forthcoming project.

Phase three: structuring phase [first part] (about three weeks)

Structuring is divided into two parts for ease of teaching. The first part focuses on understanding, planning and developing all aspects of the assessment task.

Groupings

The teacher, in consultation with the students, should choose the groups. The groups will remain the same during the entire process. There could be 6–8 students in mixed-ability groups or 6–8 students in ability groups.

Assessment of learning task

Students form their assessment groups to create the playbuilding essay for performance.

Assessment of learning task

Question: How do Brecht's political and artistic goals, and the themes in the text set for study, fuse with your group creating a playbuilding project?

Each group is to answer this question by way of a performance and an individual written response.

In your playbuilt essay you are to attempt to affect your spectators as if they were the readers of a senior drama written essay. So, just as in an essay, points or aspects of argument need to be made and backed up by evidence. This evidence should be acted out in the form of playbuilding. Remember your playbuilt essay should be theatrically dynamic and engaging and it should be 15–20 minutes in length.

You will be individually assessed on the following criteria:

Making the drama
- fusing your group's ideas about this topic into a playbuilding project;
- linking and integrating research in a dramatically powerful manner;
- attempting to use metaphor to provide a dramatic structure;
- demonstrating theatrical collaboration and cooperation.

Performing the drama
- demonstrating Brecht's artistic and political goals which relate to his thematic concerns in the play;
- demonstrating performance knowledge of Brecht's epic theatre techniques;

- demonstrating appropriate generalised characterisation techniques;
- demonstrating appropriate voice, movement and staging techniques;
- demonstrating how the playbuilding relates to contemporary spectators.

Reflecting on the drama
- investigating and acknowledging the significance of a theatrical historical context in shaping your playbuilding views;
- recognising and respecting the diversity of views of your peers;
- keeping a detailed workbook that complements the learning process.

Individual essay component
Individual written essays of 1,000 words will be handed in to the teacher one week after the completion of the performance. You will be assessed on the following criteria:

- answering the given question;
- linking theory and practice effectively;
- writing with a reflective, authoritative and engaging voice;
- providing a coherent and structured response;
- providing references.

The class reads the assessment, and this is followed by discussion to clarify any queries. For example, the teacher reiterates that the essay question has to be answered individually as a critical written drama essay as well as in a playbuilt performance. And that the students should:

- use the question as a stimulus for creating their performance;
- follow the structure of the improvisations they have experimented with in the last week as they begin exploring their assessment task;
- use or adapt any of the improvisations that they have previously explored and if appropriate incorporate them into their playbuilding;
- think of these improvisations as draft paragraph scenes that have key points which are supported by dramatic evidence;
- use their own and their group's written notes and/or draft essays as research material which will be incorporated into their plays on the stage floor.

> **Handy hint . . .**
> *The essay question should be generic in nature to help students explore the complexities of the text and associated material in a limited timeframe.*

It is very important in phase three to provide opportunities for the playbuilders to have control over their own learning while exploring the concept of playbuilding an essay. A useful opening activity would be for each group to create a 30-second dramatic response to the question using their research and extracts from the play. The group decides which epic theatre techniques to incorporate into this dramatic response to the question. The dramatic response is shown to the rest of the class to allow purposeful discussion that will broaden their knowledge of the different ways groups can go about the task. This could be followed by groups creating an opening paragraph scene. Each group discusses what topic sentence can give dramatic shape and information to their ideas. For example, a group could decide that its topic sentence is *Brecht does not intend the spectators to admire Mother Courage's courage*. This topic sentence could be projected onto a scenic backdrop and the group acts out the points they want to make.

Planning and structuring the task

After initial workshops to help begin their process, each group needs to develop their own performance essay plan to build from. The playbuilding an essay task can be planned by the group through creating a mindmap, or a diagram that connects various strands together, or by just jotting down in a linear fashion how they want to go about this task. It is important for the teacher to see every group's playbuilt essay plan and to help them refine it. Of course, this plan will most probably be altered as the playbuilding progresses, but it initially gives the group guidance.

For example, the following plan created by one group of students gives them direction and allows the teacher to monitor how they are progressing:

Group 1 – Planning our task
- This is how our group wants to go about the task of playbuilding an essay.
- We think our overriding message/story to the audience will be that nothing Brecht wrote or thought about was neutral; everything had a purpose and a reason.
- Each one of the dot points we envisage as a paragraph/scene or maybe just a dramatic moment, and we have not thought how to link anything yet.
- Perhaps open with an image of the question which we bring to life.
- One student could step into role metaphorically becoming the play; perhaps this idea could be the overriding metaphor if it works out in rehearsals.
- Maybe create some banners and/or film something relevant that tells how our story answers the question; this could be a scenic drop on our stage.
- We most probably now need a scene on how Brechtian theatre can make an audience think about relevant issues. We could back this up with a small piece of text from *Mother Courage and Her Children*.
- Then each one of us personifies a Brechtian practice which actively comments on war and his ideologies.
- We should then reshape one of the improvisations we explored in class, maybe the one about the importance of dialectics.
- Where to next? The rest of our play will develop and continue with research, but we need to start improvising now.

Another important teaching aspect is for the groups to divide up the specific research tasks that need to be undertaken. For example, a couple of students might want to research the importance of historification, other students might wish to research the epic designer and previous designs for the play. This research is brought back to the group and is used as improvisation material. The improvisations could be developed into paragraph scenes by finding a topic sentence. Eventually all these scenes are linked together as a coherent whole using their performance essay plan.

> **Handy hint . . .**
> *If some groups find the words topic sentence or paragraph scene confronting, then just ask them to create scenes that have a major dramatic point to them.*

Phase three: structuring phase [second part] (about one week)

In the second part of this phase the groups are working on solving difficulties, refining metaphor and individually working on their draft essay.

Solving difficulties

The teacher will most probably have a good idea of what problems are occurring, but it is also important to ask the groups so that detailed teaching strategies can be thought about to help groups solve issues. For example, groups may experience such problems as:

- Forgetting to add in some of Brecht's political goals such as his scrutiny of mother-hood. If this is the case the teacher could set up an improvisation such as a tug of war, symbolising a mother as a businesswoman in times of war, versus a mother who cares for and protects her children in times of war. The action for this improvisation could be in slow motion which would allow the group time to think about their dramatic meaning rather than rushing into solving their dilemma. A narrator, in role as Bertolt Brecht, could be nominated to comment on the political goals he wanted for this scene on motherhood.

or

- Forgetting to add in important artistic goals such as gestus. The teacher reminds the students that gestus is a physical gesture with attitude that provokes debate among the spectators (Thomson 1997). The teacher asks the groups to explore Scene five where Mother Courage is firmly telling the soldiers that unless they have money they cannot buy any brandy:

  Mother Courage: It's simple, I tell you. No money, no brandy.

  (Brecht 1996, p.51)

The groups should ask themselves:

- Who is the dialogue of use to?
- What practical action corresponds to it?
- What sort of response results from the action and attitude?
- What are our ideas about the importance of gestus in our playbuilding?

The groups could improvise becoming a collective Mother Courage, saying the dialogue in unison and using moneybags, with attitude, to create gestus by snapping them shut at pertinent moments.

After each one of these problem-solving activities, the teacher should remind the groups to use and expand on these improvisations and to incorporate their versions into their project.

Metaphor

Some problems may occur because groups have not attempted to create a metaphor for the playbuilding or because the metaphor they have created is overriding the playbuilding. The metaphor is important only if they can find one that provides dramatic coherence. For example, metaphors that could provide dramatic coherence are:

- A metaphorical *Brechtian surgery* where Bertolt Brecht dissects society and creates new ways to impart knowledge through his play *Mother Courage and Her Children* and its associated themes.
- A *wagon*, as a metaphoric place, in which Bertolt Brecht keeps all his artistic and political goals, and out of the wagon spills his epic theatre practices, some of which are evidenced from his play *Mother Courage and Her Children*.

Individual essay writing

Throughout phases two and three, writing strategies are introduced and developed to help students write individual draft essays from their class experiences and in response to the question. The students should be reminded that there should be a real sense of their workshops and personal explorations in these individual essays, and that they can write from the first person (I), write from their groups' perspective (we), and write from a spectator's perspective (they) as well as using such phrases as:

- My research into gestus was actively explored when . . .
- Our group improvised a dialectical scene which . . .
- My workshop experiences into the play . . .
- We worked with each other to create . . .
- As playbuilders we explored . . .

Class time should also be given to help the students plan and write the introductory paragraph, group and sub-group their arguments, find words and phrases from their improvisations to help link their arguments, synthesise their knowledge into paragraphs, and draft a conclusion.

The teacher helps students edit their individual draft essays and asks them to share their work from these essay drafts with their playbuilding group as there may be ideas in them that could be incorporated into the performance task.

Phase four: performative phase (about two weeks)

When refining the performance some groups will add paragraphs/scenes to the playbuilt essay through improvisation; others will write down their final ideas and then actively explore them, and others will go back to their original playbuilding essay plan. Each group will approach the performance completion phase in their own unique way but they will need a checklist to ensure they have covered all the pertinent areas. The checklist is a synthesis of all information that they have been exploring during the past six weeks.

> Checklist
> *Remember Brecht believed that every single thing had a purpose and nothing was wasted.*
>   Here is a checklist to help your group know if you have covered all the performance areas you are supposed to and to help you individually complete your written essay. Has your group, and your individual essay, dramatically incorporated and discussed:
>
> * your group's ideas about this topic;
> * Brecht's artistic and political goals;
> * the function and purpose of epic theatre;
> * generalised characters and the associated acting techniques;
> * the appropriate use of staging, lights, scenery, costumes, and props;
> * how Brecht sought to bring large and complex events onto the stage;
> * how this play relates to political themes of contemporary spectators;
> * evidence that backs up your ideas;
> * a dramatic metaphor to create a dramatic structure.

The groups will refine their playbuilding during intense rehearsal times where peer and teacher feedback, on their performance skills, and interpretation of the task, are invaluable. The playbuilding an essay task is performed in front of given spectators, such as their peers, friends and family, and after the performance feedback is given.

The individual written essay should be handed in a few days after the performance. This gives time for the students to incorporate their performance experience as well as to refine their personal reflections and to evaluate how playbuilding an essay has helped them to understand the nexus between Bertolt Brecht's practices, the play *Mother Courage and Her Children*, and devising their own work, and how this has flowed through to their individual experiential essay writing.

The teaching strategies in *playbuilding an essay* enhance drama students' imagining and creating. The strategies open up doors to individual essay writing skills that many drama students once felt difficult to grasp, but can now achieve, as well as introducing students to a new form of playbuilding. The combination of the group, the individual, the task and the teaching strategies creates a climate that excites and interests the students, but it is very important for the teacher to complete the unit of work by asking themselves evaluative questions such as:

* How did I structure the unit of work so that the students did not just regurgitate the ideas of the playwright, play and research material into the playbuilding project?
* Was my assessment task constructed so that I provided my students with a vibrant combined playbuilding and written experience?

- How was I opening up learning spaces so that my students' personal drama experiences could be included in their playbuilding and written drama essays?
- How was I providing openings for students to use their experiential drama knowledge, skills and understanding in their written drama essays?
- How would I do it differently when I do it again?

Chapter 8

Working with narrative

This chapter offers teachers multiple starting points and approaches for playbuilding using storying processes, narrative structures and stories as the core focus. Storying plays such a significant role in playbuilding and drama generally, and it is often so encompassing and embedded in the work that drama teachers find it hard to differentiate how narrative form is being used and developed within the drama creative process. This chapter aims to give some guidance about possible ways of using narrative forms and processes within the playbuilding process. It also offers teachers an array of approaches and ideas that can be adapted to units of work for students of all stages and levels of ability. At the same time, the chapter flags some of the critical pedagogical issues and concerns for drama educators working with narrative forms and processes in classroom playbuilding.

THE IMPORTANCE OF STORYING AND STORIES

Human beings live storied lives. Much of what we do, feel or recount takes a narrative form or turn. Barbara Hardy (1968, p. 5) suggested narrative should not to be regarded as an aesthetic invention used by artists to control, manipulate and order experience, but as a primary act of mind transferred to art from life (1968, p. 5). The act of storying helps us make sense of our experiences. Hardy says we live our lives through story:

> We dream in narrative, remember, anticipate, hope, despair, believe, doubt, plan, revise, criticize, construct, gossip, learn, hate and love by narrative. In order to really live, we make up stories about ourselves and others, about the personal as well as the social past and future.
>
> (1968, p. 5)

The process of telling stories or linking events and experiences into storied forms are central to our sense of who we are in our lived contexts and our stories evoke the textures and meanings of living. Through narrative we learn our language, our connections to family and community, our culture and our heritage. Through the act of storying we learn about ourselves and negotiate our place in the world in relationship with those who help shape our world. As Noddings and Witherell (1991, p. 1) suggest:

> Stories and narrative, whether personal or fictional, provide meaning and belonging in our lives. They attach us to others and to our own histories by providing a tapestry

rich with threads of time, place, character and even advice on what we might do with our lives. The story fabric offers us images, myths, and metaphors that are morally resonant and contribute to both our knowing and our being known.

Human knowledge is embedded in our stories and also shaped through the act of storying. Storying is linked to our sense of becoming as well as our being in this world. As a reflective action, the act of storying sustains us and allows us to enter into a caring relation with all the parts of our selves.

(Noddings 1984)

We make meaning of our lives as we reflect on experiences in a narrative fashion. Narrative psychologist Donald Polkinghorne (1988, p.1) refers to the cognitive process of narrative meaning making as a way of organising human experiences into temporally meaningful episodes. We each have our own ongoing life stories to live by. The daily stories we tell may only be a fragment of the whole story, it is fashioned by memory and context and implies the turns and twists our story may take in the future. The act of narrating is driven by our human desire for coherence and meaning, and involves processes of synthesis, recognition and reconciliation with a whole range of lived experiences (from pleasant to the painful or oppressive). Of course, stories are not created in a vacuum. They are shaped by purpose, context and history as well as place and audience. They are influenced by dominant discourses and subject positions, which the teller adopts, negotiates or resists as the story is told or enacted. These processes and issues are fundamentally embedded in drama learning as students tell, create and enact their stories. As such, teachers need to be aware of the way they use stories and storying and need to be clear as to how their approach is generating student learning, in ways that are safe, respectful and inclusive.

THE IMPORTANCE OF STORYING IN THE DRAMA CLASSROOM

As an intrinsic aspect of everyday life and as a literary structure or form, narrative and storying infuse the drama learning process. In many ways drama teachers help students to understand stories from the inside out by enabling students to devise, structure, deconstruct, enact and stage stories within their classroom dramas. As a collaborative and enactive art form, drama can breathe life into stories as students create and step inside fictional contexts and narratives and use the symbolic languages of the art form to embody them in action. With its capacity for staging stories, drama can reinterpret and re-present stories, so that we can see them anew or differently. In drama we often use stories as the focal points for exploration, improvisation and structuring dramas, where characters, situations and given circumstances within the story provide the parameters for enactment. The art form of drama can also offer students ways to reinterpret familiar stories or interweave multiple stories through a complex use of dialogue, symbol and action, creating new possibilities or revisions to old stories.

Meaning making is a central focus of the learning process in drama, where students manipulate the art form to interrogate, represent and reflect upon:

- their own and others' real-life stories and experiences;

- the original fictional stories they devise with their peers;
- the stories embedded in pre-texts, images and playtexts from a range of historical and cultural contexts.

Unlike in the study of stories in English, in drama stories are to be enacted and framed symbolically in action. Stories are lifted and brought alive through the manipulation of the dramatic art form. The dramatic elements provide students with ways to analyse and re-present aspects of the story in a collaborative embodied process.

EXPERIMENTING WITH STORYING AND NARRATIVE STRUCTURE

Learning how to create, tell and stage fictional stories

Encouraging students to create and tell stories is critical to becoming more proficient at playbuilding. Often students get limited exposure to storytelling or creating their own stories from scratch. Sometimes students are despondent about storying because it can be linked to literacy issues and problems. In drama it is important to remind students that many cultures have fine oral traditions and telling stories is a fundamental part of our lives, therefore they already have much knowledge about stories and storytelling to bring to their drama work. In playbuilding students need to have a sense on the floor of what makes an interesting story and how to tell a good story; these understandings inform the choices they make in their playbuilding projects.

Small group activities that help students experiment with storying in accessible and playful ways are:

- one word at a time stories;
- sentence at a time stories;
- telling/improvising fictional stories in pairs, where the listener acts as a coach, interjecting to ask the teller to extend or advance their story at key moments or when interesting ideas arise;
- narrated stories where the group enacts and personifies the elements of the story;
- stories in particular styles or genres – fairy tale, horror, romance, action, fantasy, biography, science fiction and others;
- stories told from different perspectives or voices – first-person, second-person or third-person, or inside the action, a witness to the action, or implicated in the action on stage.

PLAYING WITH DIFFERENT TYPES OF STORIES AND NARRATIVE STRUCTURES

The term narrative structure refers to the way a story is organised or presented to an audience (usually the reader in literary texts). It is the skeletal framework or architecture around which the ideas, events, time and space are strategically placed and patterned. Like dramatists working with dramatic structures, the writer or teller of the narrative considers how the structural and language elements work together for a particular effect or impact, often in a cause and effect-type pattern. There are many types of narrative structures and genres that have been studied in various fields such as film studies, literary theory, linguistics, semiotics and narratology (the study of narrative structure itself). In drama work we tap into a whole range of narrative structures and play with them in a live and embodied way. While there are dramatic narrative structures in various forms of literature (such as poetry or novels), in the theatre the dramatic structure of a play considers all the live, embodied, temporal and production elements as well and how they dynamically connect and add to the event of that live performance. This is why dramatists tend to see stories and their elements or indeed texts in more fluid, experiential and interpretive ways, particularly when considering characters, action, signs and the aesthetics of performance.

There are a number of basic narrative structures that could become the basis for designing playbuilding experiences. Some possible narrative structures to play with could be:

- the traditional hill or triangle structure: beginning, followed by rising action, climax, falling action, then the end;
- cumulative stories or climactic stories in a linear pattern;
- non-linear, episodic or abstract/postmodern narratives;
- problem resolution stories;
- days of the week stories or diarised structures;
- circular stories;
- journey or travel stories;
- hero's quest;
- single event stories, same event presented a number of times.

Handy hint . . .

The narrative triangle or pyramid was developed by German writer Gustav Freytag in 1863, when analysing Aristotle's Poetics. *It is a common structure used in narratives and school students are often taught to construct stories primarily in this way.*

Other possible story forms useful for playbuilding could be:

- participatory stories, where the audience is directly engaged at key moments (good children's theatre or pantomime would be useful for students to consider);
- stories that exaggerate the truth, e.g. tall stories, witness stories, stories told by objects at the scene (personification);
- biographies or autobiographies;
- stories that are created around specific objects, places, emotions, foods (to be served in performance or recipes can be printed to accompany the performance);
- intergenerational stories – told by various generations either live, recorded or using voice-overs and other visual images;
- stories that play with elements of chance, notions of time, juxtaposition of contrasting scenes or disconnected episodes;
- radio drama – this is a whole form of drama that can be studied in its own right. Digital technologies offer interesting possibilities for publishing and sharing radio plays in new and exciting ways (e.g. podcasting).

Thanks to developments in digital media, technologies and gaming fields, narrative form is in itself shifting and these developments are also impacting the way narrative form is created, structured and manipulated. Janet H. Murray, in her book *Hamlet on the Holodeck: The Future of Narrative in Cyberspace* (1997), offers an interesting discussion of the way narrative forms are changing and becoming more multiple, complex and sophisticated. Storying in the immersive worlds of games and the internet means that our students have a much more dynamic sense of narrative form and structure than teachers perhaps realise. These understandings and sensibilities can be activated through playbuilding, where students can use the art form to embody and create virtual worlds in performance. Chapter 9 gives teachers further ideas on how to tailor the playbuilding process to incorporate technologies.

GETTING INSIDE A STORY: TEACHING IDEAS FOR PLAYBUILDING WITH A NARRATIVE FOCUS

There are many starting points for drama that imply a story context or structure either explicitly or implicitly. Drama teachers will often gather examples of good starting points or pre-texts from which to design units of work and sometimes they will use one starting point in quite different ways with different groups of students. Text-based starting points such as poems, stories and lyrics are filled with narrative threads and dramatic possibilities for the teacher to use for the purposes of drama learning. In the initial phases of planning a teacher will approach the task both creatively and tangentially, brainstorming the possible dramatic leads in terms of the fictional context presented. The teacher works like a director or dramaturg, deconstructing the text for possible trajectories of learning, looking for ideas or moments where students can bring their own creative interpretations to their playbuilding. Teachers could consider:

- key ideas/meanings that could be drawn from the work as a whole;
- possible roles to be explored – inside the text, outside the text, implied by the text;
- the fictional contexts or worlds presented that could be dramatised, enacted and constructed in the space;
- the key dramatic moments of action that could be explored;
- symbols that could be experimented within the drama work, either mentioned in the piece itself or that could be used to focus the drama;
- implied points of focus or tension in the piece and possible departures from those points;
- elements that are evocative or poetic or aesthetically interesting that could inform the playbuilding process and be explored further;
- possible pathways for narrative investigation, storylines to pursue in the drama.

AN EXAMPLE OF TEACHER PLANNING FOR NARRATIVE PLAYBUILDING

There are many ways teachers can begin their planning for creating new units of work. Here is one possible approach to playbuilding with a story focus using the poem 'The

Loner' by Julie Holder. This example shows the way teachers might meet the text and begin to develop their ideas for planning a playbuilding project. Approaching starting points creatively in the first phase of planning allows the teacher to sense the starting point's potential for generating strong drama learning experiences.

The Loner

He leans against the playground wall,
Smacks his hands against the bricks
And other boredom-beating tricks,
Traces patterns with his feet,
Scuffs to make the tarmac squeak
Back against the wall he stays—
And never plays.
The playground's quick with life,
The beat is strong.
Though sharp as a knife
Strife doesn't last long.
There is shouting, laughter, song,
And a place at the wall
For who won't belong.
We pass him running, skipping, walking,
In slow huddled groups, low talking.
Each in our familiar clique
We pass him by and never speak,
His loneness is his shell and shield
And neither he nor we will yield.
He wasn't there at the wall today,
Someone said he'd moved away
To another school and place
And on the wall where he used to lean
Someone has chalked
'watch this space'.

                                    Julie Holder, 1982

Why is this a good starting point?

It is useful to consider first why you as the drama teacher want to use this particular starting point for a playbuilding project. Questions the teacher could consider are:

- What types of learning could be generated from using this piece and why would those types of learning be important for the class doing the project?
- What key ideas are represented in this poem?
- What type of response does it evoke in you? What do you sense and imagine? What do you want to know more about? What is implied?

- What narrative threads or tangents could be explored dramatically from this piece? Do these imply any particular dramatic or narrative structures that could be used?
- What human issues does this piece consider? What does it make significant or foreground in terms of themes, problems or human experience?

This starting point is an excellent one for playbuilding because it could be used with different age groups, who would bring quite different approaches, ideas and life experiences to the creative process. For instance, younger students may want to focus more broadly on the notion of bullying that is implied in the text; middle teens may wish to explore space, isolation and loneliness whereas older students may wish to explore these with further depth and complexity, even adding layers such as social class or cultural differences to the piece to explore issues of belonging and schooling in more critical ways.

The teacher might then respond to the work and begin to articulate the aspects that could be investigated through playbuilding. The example in the figure below shows how one teacher has met the text in this way (Figure 8.1).

Key ideas or themes	belonging inclusion/exclusion childhood	schooling loneness or loneliness power
Roles and relationships	*Inside the text* – the loner, the other children (from active bullies to passive witnesses), the graffiti artist	
	Implied by the text – teachers & school personnel, parents, community members, other witnesses, past and future loners	
	Outside the text – counsellors, police, future families of these children when they become adults, researchers of behaviour or schools	
Fictional contexts and worlds	The playground – in reality or as a more abstract space	
	The world inside the minds of the key characters	
	Real world that becomes another world – a nightmare world, or a battleground or a dolls house	
	This school – what type is it? Where is it?	
Key dramatic moments	Break time at this school – patterns that recur, waiting/beating boredom and loneliness	
	Moments when the contrasts are the strongest – when the life and liveliness of the playground are strong, compared with stillness and micro-world of the loner.	
	When the children passing him/her by – what happens?	
	Implied moment – the moment the loner leaves the school	
Symbols	The wall	
	The tarmac	
	Child's play/games	
	Graffiti	

Points of focus or tension	Relationship between the loner and the group of children – how that is choreographed in the space, where they almost meet or connect and how that happens, the effects
	The loner as a central focus in the space, perhaps through contrasting movement or isolation within the space
	The ambivalence of adults to this scene
Evocative elements	The space and how it is inhabited, balancing movement and stillness/sound and silence and how these represent the play of power in this setting
	The idea of the playground (and childhood) as being happy and innocent and participatory
Possible storylines to explore	*The loner's backstory* – where did this loner come from? What brought him/her here?
	The loner's future story – how does he/she remember their childhood/his old school? When might he have to revisit this, where did he go – e.g. reunions, talking to his/her own children about their schooling? What happened after they left that school? As an adult, how does he/she remember experience?
	The loner's present story – who is he/she? What are their thoughts/experiences each day? Why do they leave? Where did they go?
	The stories of that playground – past and future loners, past and future powerful people, teachers' stories
Possible dramatic techniques to experiment with	Playing with time – rewinds/fast forward
	Playing with contexts – juxtaposition/counter-narratives/public and private contexts, parallel action
	Playing with style – realism, abstract, expressionism, surreal
	Experimenting with the actor/audience relationship – in the space, one of the children, participatory elements of the work, the audience as witnesses, considering ways to enhance empathy
	Experimenting with sound, voice, silence, repetition and emphasis, music and song
	Experimenting with movement – stylization, repetition, space
	Experimenting with objects of significance – a school bag, a pair of glasses, a veil, a doll
	Playing with design – lighting, costume, staging, imagery (for example, using photographs and projections to amplify the stage action or create complexity or add layers to the scenes).

Figure 8.1 A teacher's response to the poem 'The Loner'

From here the teacher combines their ideas and organises them in a possible sequence that constructs learning experiences which enable the students to explore and create in an organised and progressive fashion. In making their decisions about sequencing and structuring the unit the teacher keeps their aims and intended learning outcomes in mind, to ensure the work is both engaging for students and also generative in terms of drama learning. Care also needs to be given to how the core practices of making, performing and reflecting are used throughout the unit.

STAGING OUR STORIES USING PERSONAL NARRATIVE FOR PLAYBUILDING

Working with students' personal narratives in drama

Personal narratives offer rich territory for the artistic process for playbuilding. In seeking out personal narratives for exploration in drama, we invite the narrative meaning making of each individual into the learning process of the group and into their creative process. In doing so the playbuilding becomes a dynamisation of narrative meaning making as the individuals in the group tell and collectively dramatise their stories. In doing so, the playbuilding process makes each person's individual narrative meaning making enactive, embodied and, more importantly, shared. Through this type of playbuilding, the drama form can capture momentarily the subject in transition, or as Kristeva (1981) suggests, the subject in process and can contribute to the continuous process of identity construction, informing who we are after this moment of telling and staging our story.

There are a number of critical and ethical considerations for the drama teacher using students' personal narratives as the content for playbuilding. The teacher needs to be aware of all the layers at work in the creative process. If we invite our students to use their stories to frame the drama, we invite them to activate that narrative meaning-making process, to organise and stage in story form what is significant for them, as only they see it. Storying foregrounds the personal, social, cultural and embodied knowledge students bring to the learning. Drama can be an important way to make sense of experience and encourage understanding and dialogue.

There is a significant power shift when we allow our students to become the subjects within the art form as the teacher yields their control of the content of the drama. The collaborative process in drama allows the stories to be retold in new and dynamic ways, thereby allowing a kind of re-vision to take place. Students can play with social selves and fantasy selves as they construct and negotiate within their dramas. The dramatic action can become a staged conversation students have with themselves and then with their audiences. When done well, this can be an exciting way to generate understandings on many different levels for both the playbuilders and their audience.

Stories that are shaped into dramatic form involve a more public sharing of the story than written forms. In performance the story is shared and received. It becomes significant, visible and public. Drama form can air stories and strengthen the voices of people either not normally heard or often misunderstood, enabling connection, empathy and awareness to be generated in both process and performance. This is not without its risks and teachers need to be aware of what is at stake as they invite students to use personal narratives in drama. Not all storying is intrinsically empowering or positive by nature. It can only be so if it is supported and developed in safe, negotiated and generative ways within the drama process.

Also, not all stories are happy or neatly structured. If drama teachers invite students to stage painful or traumatic stories, extreme care needs to be taken in this process; indeed it is best to consider other ways or topics that are less confronting for the student involved. Drama teachers should be careful in setting up clear parameters for student story sharing and steer clear of difficult personal terrain. Should students disclose serious issues such as self-harm or abuse during their playbuilding, the teacher has a duty of care to follow appropriate channels and procedures for dealing with disclosures of this kind. Just because such things surface in drama does not alter the teacher's responsibility to notify appropriate school managers and take steps to support the student, beyond the drama process itself.

No drama process should force or pressure students to tell their stories. All storying should be invited and voluntary. Sometimes inexperienced drama teachers will push students to tell their stories without a carefully structured process or specific strategies to frame the telling to provide safety, respite and/or distancing through the dramatic process. Often such difficult stories are way beyond the lived experience or cultural knowledge of the teacher and there is a real danger of exoticising the story and its teller in terms of culture, race and ethnicity.

As stories are fashioned into performance they are mediated by the art form. Teachers need to guide students carefully when considering how personal stories will be represented onstage. Careful use of dramatic elements, structure and sign will guard against cultural tourism or colonising or appropriating those stories. Drama teachers need to consider their own purpose and agenda in staging particular students' stories within their school contexts and for particular audiences. The students' safety and learning should be the teacher's prime focus. It is important to remember that personal narratives do not usually have an ending; they are part of students' ongoing life stories. If the storyteller is a class member, their life story continues well beyond the moment of telling. To tell, share and perform their stories, students need to negotiate the boundaries of safety and risk in the process.

Students' stories are also connected to their own personal contexts, which means family, friends and communities may feature as characters in their stories. The teacher needs to manage and mediate these connections so that key people do not feel exposed or compromised in the way they are framed in the stories or the plays as they are performed. How are significant others framed and represented in both the story and its performance? In what ways are they present in the work – as characters (onstage or off), as onstage images (projected photographs, or physically in movement or in freezes) or in dialogue (voices, text, subtext)? Some students will also use the storying process to construct alternative or more agentive versions of themselves and/or their experiences, particularly if there are friendship issues within the class. Drama work operates at the nexus between reality and fiction, where students play with performances of self and social dynamics. For some groups the teacher may need to explicitly teach students to tell and, more importantly, to listen and receive others' stories, and set up protocols around the process. Students do not want personal details or stories retold outside the drama classroom, in ways that discriminate against or bully the story owner. Trust and respect for each other needs to be reinforced by the teacher at every step of the process. Good drama teachers strategically build reflective and respectful drama cultures at every opportunity, to ensure this is a key part of the pedagogical architecture of all drama processes.

Another issue for the teacher to be mindful of is that students' personal narratives are informed by broader social, cultural storylines, discourses and histories, which need to be considered with sensitivity as students share and enact their own stories. Key questions for the teacher are:

- What stories need to be told and why?
- How are students to make sense of difficult intersections and complex storylines through their playbuilding?

It is worth remembering that students are young at life as well as being young at art. As people, they are also more than the sum of their stories. As the leader of the playbuilding process, it is the teacher who needs to support the students' growing understandings about their own stories and selves as they playbuild. If students' stories are characterised by experiences of disenfranchisement or social disadvantage, then the teacher needs to help them find ways to communicate their stories with clarity but also with hope, empathy and humanity. The wonderful nature of our art form is its elasticity and the ways in which we can use its symbolic languages to communicate ideas in artful ways. Teachers need to juggle all of these perspectives and issues on the floor and facilitate the creative process with a sense of inclusivity and support at every step.

> **Handy hint . . .**
> For teachers wanting guidance about dealing with sensitive personal narratives in drama, useful insights can be gained from further readings in dramatherapy with young people; see the work of Renee Emunah or Sue Jennings.

As a public art form, dramatic performance makes stories and voices visible. The teacher needs to be sensitive to the ramifications of this process. Not all school contexts and communities are ready to or interested in hearing or seeing the stories of young people and how they live their lives enacted in performance. Schools are not always places that encourage students to share their views or stories of lived experiences. Drama offers processes and spaces to empower students to consider their own stories and lives as valuable and worth staging; however, drama teachers need to understand that students' stories, when performed, may also challenge or provoke confrontation with adults and community-based audiences. This should be considered during the playbuilding process and the work needs to be made with the potential audiences' views and values in mind.

> **Handy hint . . .**
> A useful text to read that assists drama teachers in understanding the ways in which cultural studies impact dramatic processes and interpretations is Kathleen Berry's The Dramatic Arts and Cultural Studies (2000).

Here are some ideas for a teaching unit where students' stories are used as the content for playbuilding. In this work, the focus on the devising process encourages students to use the stories rather than delve too deeply or personally into them. A structured process enables students to work creatively but with sufficient distance from the story. Throughout the process the teacher would need to check and monitor the playbuilding to ensure the story owners are comfortable with the way the group is working and the interpretations being made along the way.

A possible playbuilding process could be:

1   The teacher constrains the process by giving the work a central theme which allows students to contain their storying and consider their positioning in relation to that

theme (e.g. childhood, celebrations, girlhood/boyhood, family, food, song, starting school, etc.).

2   Exploring the cultural currency of the theme – brainstorming about connotations, images, stereotypes, behaviours, issues connected with the theme.

3   Doing research connected with the theme – surveys, vox pops, interviews.

4   Making scenes about the effects of the cultural currency on an individual's choices/experiences – e.g. stylised scenes, machines, realistic scenes, before and after scenes.

5   Collecting students' views through one-liners, statements, video bytes.

6   Gathering ideas via memory boxes/other collections of ephemera.

7   Writing stories as monologues.

8   Using a mix of digital storying and live performance – how do the images and action intersect or overlap or contradict each other?

9   Considering place and feelings – how our memories are linked to place and bodily experience, e.g. travel, playgrounds, accidents, strong experiences. Considering how we evoke places on our stories.

10   Group representation of stories – how can one story be embodied and communicated by a whole group? What techniques can enhance the story (such as movement, sound, and dialogue, using the stage space to manipulate focus, tension and mood)? Consider the way music might underscore the work.

11   Weaving the stories into one play – layering stories, connecting through linking ideas, doubling dialogue or character, using symbols in different ways, finding points where stories intersect or overlap, giving the work a structure.

12   Performing the play – for different-aged audiences, in different spaces for different purposes, e.g. a community centre, a library, on the street, to celebrate youth week, as a stimulus for meetings or discussions between educators or community members about youth issues.

OTHER POSSIBILITIES OF PLAYBUILDING WITH PERSONAL NARRATIVES

In recent years there has been an explosion of interest in narrative uses and possibilities. Traces of study and experimentation in narrative can be found in:

- therapy (narrative and drama therapies);
- community development (oral history projects and verbatim theatre);
- applied theatre (theatre for development, youth theatre, theatre in health settings, museum theatre, prison theatre);
- research (narrative inquiry, ethnodrama, arts-based research, performed ethnography, collective memory work);
- film and video drama;
- online games and immersive environments on the internet.

In theatre there has been a growing interest in storytelling and forms such as playback theatre, verbatim theatre, feminist theatre, postcolonial theatre, theatre of the oppressed, community theatre, reminiscence theatre, that have used stories and storying in fresh new ways, for different purposes and audiences. Teachers may be interested in exploring some of these possibilities in terms of what they offer for potential approaches to playbuilding.

Important note . . .

The ethical, dramatic and pedagogical tensions and sensitivities mentioned earlier regarding using students' stories for playbuilding also apply to any project where students are collecting other people's stories as material for devising. Students would need to be briefed and monitored if they use other people's stories for their drama work. Students would need to collect and use the stories in ways that are respectful of the story owner and their sensitivities and the contexts involved.

PLAYBUILDING WITH CULTURAL WORKS AND STORIES

Cultural works such as art works, objects, rituals, myths and stories offer wonderfully rich starting points for playbuilding. They also generate important intercultural understandings as students engage with and explore the symbolic languages and meanings associated with the work or story. These types of works encourage students to investigate the parallels between people of different places, races and cultures, but also engage with the exciting differences the work or story opens up for investigation and celebration. Working with cultural artefacts or stories in drama and particularly in playbuilding requires an approach that is open, accepting and investigative. There is a danger of using and appropriating cultural works or stories with little reference to their original context, purpose and meaning. Teachers have to be careful to steer students away from cultural tourism or working with stories and artefacts in ways that are not respectful of the people, cultural knowledges, traditions and practices they represent.

In selecting a cultural starting point for playbuilding the drama teacher would also consider the type of creative process and the learning it might generate. Time needs to be given to helping the students become acquainted with the work and the culture it is drawn from, before they can work with it in their playbuilding. To do this, students might:

- Interview people from their own schools or communities about their culture or the work itself. If there are students within the class from the same cultural background, teachers will need to ensure they are comfortable with the process and not necessarily expected to be cultural experts. It is important that no student feels they are being put on the spot in this way; they should have the right to opt out and not be the focus if they so wish. Students who have membership of the cultural work being used have a very different perspective and relationship to the work than those students from different backgrounds.
- Do research in books, movies and on the internet to look at the histories, beliefs, places and practices that inform that work or story.
- Seek expert advice from cultural elders, leaders and artists from that culture. It is exciting for students to learn songs, dances and stories first-hand if they can, engaging in live and embodied ways rather than as viewers.

If using stories of cultural significance, attention needs to be given to the protocols surrounding use of the stories. There may be issues of ownership and custodianship of stories that need to be observed before stories can be reimagined in the devising process. Often in cultures with oral traditions of storytelling and ceremony, stories are positioned within a matrix of cultural practices and rules, which need to be understood. It is possible that to rework some stories in drama would be inappropriate to the given culture and its people. Particularly sensitive stories are often those which contain religious or cultural beliefs or ceremonial significance. It is important not to appropriate or offend cultural groups by allowing students to challenge or reinterpret stories without a full and reasoned understanding of the terrain.

Consideration and sensitivity need to be given not only to the selection of stories to be used, but also to the way stories and works are to be used within the drama process. How the work will be represented, by what means and for what intention are all key questions for the teacher and students to consider before they begin to playbuild. Students will need to ensure they do not work in ways that are disrespectful or ignorant of the works, their owners and the original purposes, meanings or contexts of the work. Students will also need to think about their intended audience and how their own play might enhance further intercultural understandings.

There are many excellent types of cultural works that can be used as starting points for playbuilding. Possible starting points could be:

- poems – historic, contemporary, poems of particular types;
- songs and music – traditional or contemporary, folk music, music with a purpose (e.g. marching music or ballads);
- visual art such as paintings, drawings, sculpture and photographs;
- cultural dances such as those for individuals or for groups, or dances that tell stories;
- rituals and ceremonies that map rites of passage, that make offerings, that assist in prayer or meditation, or daily rituals;
- cultural objects or artefacts – costume, items associated with work or the home or migration, shoes, cooking objects, nets, spears, shells;
- food and celebrations – connected with cultural events or festivals, or family practices;
- children's stories – tales for teaching children lessons for living, children's picture books, games, toys and songs.

USING FOLK TRADITIONS FROM AROUND THE WORLD FOR PLAYBUILDING

If teachers use folktales as the basis for playbuilding, it is critical that students have an understanding of the cultural and story traditions the tale is drawn from, as this will inform their own devising process. Possible playbuilding projects could involve:

- staging the tale – in a traditional or contemporary way;
- considering key figures or characters within the tale;
- reappraising cultural stories, considering their meanings for young people today;
- exploring different points of view or juxtaposing ideas and images from the same or different tales;

- considering place, climate and history and how they inform the tale or its telling now.

Teachers have a whole range of folktale traditions to draw upon for playbuilding from all corners of the globe. Unfortunately, because of the predominance and currency of Western culture, its folk traditions tend to dominate in terms of literature and film. There are, however, many rich and diverse traditions to be found in cultures and regions throughout the world, which have many stories worth using for playbuilding in the classroom. Some possible folk traditions to tap into:

- ancient tales for teaching or handing down the cultural knowledge and practices – aboriginal stories such as Australian, North American, Inuit cultures; Greek myths; Roman stories; Jewish tales;
- regional stories and traditions – Arabic, Pacific Island, European, African, Asian, Nordic, Latino, Celtic;
- narrative poetry and song from around the world;
- religious tales – from various traditions, denominations and belief systems connected with human experiences or rituals such as birth, marriage and death.

PLAYBUILDING USING MORE CONTEMPORARY STORIES

It is also possible to use more contemporary stories for playbuilding. Students can create modern folktales, that speak of their lives and experiences or those of our time. Some contexts or types of contemporary stories that students could create are:

- modern folktales, that speak of their lives and experiences;
- stories from postcolonial places;
- urban stories;
- rural stories;
- immigrant tales and refugee stories;
- stories influenced by postmodernism and digital technologies in terms of content, image and structure;
- stories of/from/within war zones;
- stories of protest;
- stories for peace.

Students may also consider creating plays that tell stories of contemporary life, perhaps considering:

- clashes of cultures;
- the impact of globalisation on lives;
- problems of belonging or making/sustaining communities;
- the impact of world events on individual lives;
- the differences in stories from different people in different locations layered so as to create plays with a focus on political commentary or debate.

PLAYBUILDING WITH THE WESTERN FAIRYTALE TRADITION: CREATING YOUR OWN FAIRY TALE

Unit description

Many films and games that students know are informed by the Western fairytale traditions. These traditions make interesting starting points for playbuilding and students of all ages often already have an understanding of the way this tradition works. Here is an example of a teaching unit that demonstrates how teachers might encourage students to engage with Western fairytale traditions and create their own plays from them.

Fairy tales and their associated motifs are known by school students of all ages, societies and cultures.

In this unit of work the playbuilders are given the opportunity to use the metaphoric structure of fairy tales to create plays about the human condition. This playbuilding is an opportunity for students to explore forces in their society such as religion, science, power, or the family through manipulating the key motifs. The way the playbuilders devise their plays will emerge from their interests and maturity; it is important to make sure that the students do not copy a known fairy tale, but devise their own. Furthermore, the groups will be small, three being the preferred size, which creates opportunities to teach them about transformational acting.

> *Handy hint . . .*
> *Useful textbooks are K. Canton's* The Fairy Tale Revisited *(1994) and V. Propp's* Theory and History of Folklore *(1984).*

How long?

Suggested timeline is 6 weeks based on 4 × 50-minute lessons.

Phase one: generative phase (about one week)

The teacher opens the playbuilding project by advising the class that they are going to collaborate in devising a play using the structure of fairy tales. In this first week of exploration it is important for students to discover that fairy tales have key motifs, which means they have recurring patterns such as often-repeated ideas, archetypical characters, and similar themes and rhythms in their construction. The teacher asks the students to find a place alone in the classroom where they sit or stand in the neutral position with their eyes closed; they are going to listen to a fairy tale. They must give their imaginations over to this fairy tale, vividly filling in the gaps and creating the dramatic action in their minds.

> Imagine that you are a heroic character of about your own age that lives in an enchanted realm. Your father sends you on a quest to recover a talisman that has been stolen from your family. A villain follows you on your journey trying to stop you achieving your quest; treachery surrounds you. You meet some helpful children, whom you trust, but they unwittingly help this villain pursue you. Your life

is in great danger at all times and safety eludes you. A person with magical qualities helps you to continue on with your quest, but only after testing your valour. Eventually you recover the stolen talisman, destroy the villain, and return triumphant to your father's land.

The teacher asks the students:

- What are the key motifs in this simplistic fairy tale?
- What is the major issue of this fairy tale?
- There are a multitude of themes within this one issue, what are they?
- Why are fairy tales important in a society?

The teacher explains that many of our modern-day fairy tales (films, books and the performing arts) have weakened the original intent of such tales because more often than not everything goes right; they have been simplified to make them a palatable genre for young children. Originally fairy tales were a very ancient oral adult tradition that reflected pain, suffering, cruelty and the search for happiness. The next spiralling teaching strategy is for the students to physically respond to a fairy tale that is not sanitised but which is still located in a realm that is not known to human kind.

You are a child who has been abducted and locked away from society by a person who is extremely jealous of you. Find one gesture that speaks of your despair; now another gesture to plead for your freedom. Transform your body into the jailor and create one gesture that demonstrates why you have taken this child; now transform into a storyteller whose gesture demonstrates ambiguity as to whether this child is ever found.

The teacher leads a discussion which explores missing children as a universal tragedy that arouses powerful emotions in any society and culture. The students are asked to reveal what their character's gestures may have represented about this universal tragedy of a missing child. It might be useful to compare the contemporary fairy tale of Rapunzel, with its happy ending, with a fairy tale where the child may not be found.

In this next improvisation, focusing on key motifs, students must be fully engaged and accept all offers as well as physically extending every moment and add sounds or words when they think it is appropriate. They are asked to move around the classroom and:

- individually become *Once upon a time*;
- in groups of three *The quest*;
- individually become *An enchanted talisman*;
- in groups of five *Birth and death*;
- are divided into four groups, of which two groups become *The happy family* while the other two groups *The unhappy family*;
- are divided into four groups, of which two groups become *Evil winged messengers* and the other two groups *Good winged messengers*.

Students discuss their instinctive responses to the above key motifs and how the different active groupings affected the dramatic outcome. The discussion is that this approach steers away from theory-based acting to the bodily kinaesthetic approach.

The teacher explains that they are now going to explore archetypal characters through transformational acting. This gives students the experience of developing a number of characters without intellectualising but by using their current emotions to explore character uniqueness.

> Transformational acting means you have to engage immediately with the emotions of your body and physically bring out what it tells you about the character. You are going to become archetypal characters from fairy tales; these are universal characters that appear repeatedly in all fairy tales in all societies and cultures and are instantly recognisable throughout the world.

The students become the:

- hero
- anti-hero
- villain
- magical helper
- victim.

They discuss who became a gallant or stupid hero and why, or who became a charming or obsequious villain and why, and how they physically transformed from one archetype to another.

> **Handy hint . . .**
> The class could explore other archetypal characters such as the wicked stepmother, the fairy godmother, the youngest son, the sad princess.

During the next couple of lessons students are asked to read one fairy tale from outside their culture and one from within their culture. They bring this knowledge back to the talking circle where the teacher poses key questions so that their growing knowledge about fairy tales is deepened by collective sharing.

- What archetypal characters were in the fairy tales you read?
- How do archetypal characters embody universal meanings to an audience?
- How did these fairy tales mirror important day-to-day living situations?
- Did these fairy tales resolve issues or have unhappy or even cruel endings?

> **Handy hint . . .**
> It may be that some students have to be reminded that these tales generally do not have fairies in them but are about realms in which folkloric characters and all that live there exist.

Phase two: constructing phase (about three weeks)

Groupings

Groups of three. Small groups allow the students to experiment with transformational acting techniques as they have to take on at least two characters. Also, using uneven numbers can widen the variety of character interactions, as characters have more possibilities of changing allegiances within the play's structure.

Assessment of learning task

The following assessment *of* learning task should be given to the students at the beginning of this phase.

Assessment *of* learning task

Use this quote as a stimulus for your fairy tale-based playbuilding:

> The realm of fairy-story is wide and deep and high and filled with many things: all manner of beasts and birds are found there; shoreless seas and stars uncounted; beauty that is an enchantment, and an ever present peril; both joy and sorrow sharp as swords. In that realm a man may, perhaps, count himself fortunate to have wandered, but its very richness and strangeness tie the tongue of the traveller who would report them. And while he is there it is dangerous for him to ask too many questions, lest the gate should be shut and the keys be lost.
>
> (Tolkien 1983/2006, p.109)

In your group you are to devise an 8–10-minute fairy tale that reflects key forces in our society such as religion, science, politics, power, the family. When developing your story keep in mind that fairy tales teach us about trying to overcome adversity, finding resilience within ourselves and the ethical consequence of our actions. They are in fact a metaphor for the human condition. The criteria upon which you and your group will be assessed are:

- using transformational acting to develop and sustain two distinct archetypal characters;
- using appropriate key motifs to create dramatic coherence and structure;
- establishing a clear actor–audience relationship in the context of the performance style.

You are also required to become a theatre critic for the play created by one of your peers. You must watch this play in the final performance with a critical eye, taking notes about the plot, the themes, the characters, and the way the performers engage the audience. You must then write a 300-word theatre review discussing the key theatrical elements that created dramatic meaning using your own passionate and genuine theatre-writing voice. These reviews will be discussed in a theatre critics' meeting a week after the performance.

Before the groups of three are established, the whole class forms the talking circle and they are asked to silently read the quote from this assessment task. The teacher then opens the discussion by saying:

- How do you feel after reading that passage?
- Why do you feel this way?
- How could you use the essence of this passage in your forthcoming playbuilding project?
- What storyline structures are inherent in this passage?
- What does this passage say about the connection between fairy tales and the human condition?

When the class has discussed the passage the groups begin the task of developing their plays. At this point in time it would be useful to give the students a list of various key motifs and a generic plot structure that may help each group build a metaphoric structure for their play.

The storyline
- once upon a time
- a long time ago
- in the future
- the quest
- the happy family and/or the unhappy family
- birth and death.

Characters found in the tale
- archetypal characters
- characters with flaws
- lost children/children in distress
- inhuman characters.

Sub-structures that move the tale forward
- beauty and peril
- odd events
- enchantments
- magical animals
- talismans
- winged messengers.

Generic plot structure of a fairy tale
- A member of a family (generally the hero) leaves home with a purpose such as a quest to lift a spell, to find their future, to recover a talisman that belongs to their family.
- On the way unexpected events happen. From these events the hero may be tricked into betraying their secret. They may blame everyone but themselves for the things that have gone wrong. They may be given the opportunity to wish for something but the wish does not turn out as expected.
- They meet a villain(s), a victim(s); a magical helper(s); inhuman characters; talking animals; anti-heroes; enchanted objects. Because of these encounters demands are made of the hero that tests their integrity.

- The hero and villain have a direct confrontation that relates to the hero's quest. The hero usually wins, but on returning home there can be some disaster that awaits, or there can be a happy ending.

If the groups are disciplined enough they should be given a couple of lessons to freely explore all of their initial ideas and to start developing scenes.

Archetypical characters

During the second week of phase two the teacher runs transformational acting warm-ups that remind the students of the importance of exploring this technique while they are creating their characters and scenes.

For example, the class work together for the first 15 minutes of the lesson before they go off into their individual groups. During these 15 minutes the teacher explains that transformational acting is about working with their bodies, voices and instincts and being willing to take risks. They will be experimenting with their two archetypal characters using their creative spontaneity to express their ideas. They must remember that the transitions between the characters must be sharp, as their acting job is to create vivid, distinctive characters. Each transformation, from one character to another, will take place within a nanosecond; in this nanosecond characters pause, then transform.

> Take one of your characters for a walk. Experiment with this character's physicality. Stretch out, curl up, stride across the room, tiptoe to a corner. Imagine that you have been given a magical bottle that will protect you, if you care for it; examine it, hug it, hide it, forget about it. You now desperately need it, but it has disappeared. Blame everything and everybody else for its disappearance except yourself; freeze. Transform into your second character. Move across the room but vary the way and pace you travel; creep, slither, trot, stamp, run; put a curse on the crops; fall in love; try to commit murder; feel despair; feel great joy; freeze.
>
> Go back to the frozen position of your first archetypal character, how does this reflect your character's purpose and function in the tale. Focus on the sharpness of the physical transformation and now become your second character; what does your physicality say about this character's purpose and function in the tale?

The class discuss the notion that any member of any audience, anywhere, should consciously and unconsciously be able to recognise their developing archetypal characters and their motivations, and this should provoke powerful emotions in their future audience.

Further archetypal character techniques are to ask the groups to create a tableau from their story that demonstrates that not all is as it seems, then, what it really is; thus representing the complexity underlying the human condition. The groups should also explore the physicality of the dialogue that must respond to the dramatic needs of the different characters. For example, the students explore which character's language is intense or easy-going, flowery or taciturn; they should write a short letter to each other about their wishes and desires in their fairy tale. The groups should also explore:

- why each character is an archetype;
- what each character's relationship is to the other;
- which characters tell lies and why.

These types of strategies could be used as assessments *for* learning so that the teacher knows that the students have understood the importance of archetypal characters and transformation acting techniques and the groups could also incorporate these strategies into their developing scenes.

Motifs

It is important to help groups focus on particular motifs that help reinforce the overall meaning of their play. The teacher reminds the groups that a motif is a repeated pattern, mark, sign, a thing that represents something important.

For example, if the groups are using a talisman they must remember that it can be a motif for a quest, or to give protection or that it performs a specific task. A talisman can be a ring, a stone, a magically charged object that creates a specific force. Mainly this charged object is a protection against evil, but sometimes it can be a special weapon to enforce evil or even an object that produces extraordinary effects regardless of whether it is used to avert or create evil. Other motifs used in fairy tales are such things as magical animals like an owl who may impart some type of wisdom if only the listener can understand, or a maze or an enchanted wood that characters get lost in while trying to find their way. Motifs bring emotions from dizzying happiness to profound despair; they can both fulfil dreams and dash the hopes of the archetypal characters.

The groups should be given the freedom to play with their motifs, exploring how they are a focus that drives the tension forward, and they demonstrate this exploration to the teacher.

Make-up and costumes

This phase is taught at the teacher's discretion. If it is introduced too early, the students may get distracted, and if too late there is not enough time to experiment with make-up and costumes.

The class discuss how theatrical make-up can enhance and help to develop their archetypal characters. As the majority of the students will be taking on two characters the make-up used will be generic in its purpose and function. The basic rules the students have to follow is that all make-up is applied taking into account stage light washout on a face. This means that they need a foundation slightly darker than their normal skin colour and they may wish to highlight their natural cheekbone structure to extenuate their face. They should use eye-liner and eye-shadow to give the eyes prominence, and it might be appropriate for students to use false eyelashes; lip-liner and lipstick are also used to accentuate the mouth.

The class are given an outline of an androgenous face and are asked to alter, paint, colour and shade it to suit their generic character. This means they will have a template to follow when they are given a lesson experiment with the actual theatre make-up (see Figure 8.2).

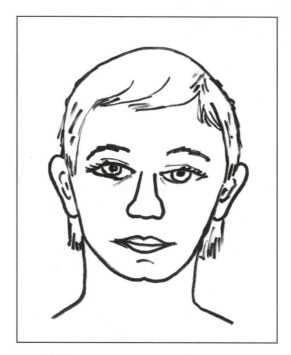

Figure 8.2 Androgenous face

Simultaneously the groups should also be exploring how to costume their archetypal characters. They will need to think carefully about creating one generic costume for both characters while using such things as hats, scarves, glasses, belts, or props to delineate from one to another.

The groups should decide:

- what style of costumes they want;
- what do they have readily accessible or what can they easily borrow or make;
- what colours and patterns do they want and what mood does this create;
- how will the costume look under the stage lighting;
- how do the costumes show the relationships between the characters.

The groups could sketch their costumed characters in their workbooks so that they get a visual idea of what they are after.

Phase three: structuring phase (about two weeks)

The teacher reminds their students that their playbuilding is metaphoric as the fairytale story and its scenic structure is a comparative device dealing with human perspectives.

The teacher explains to the class that each scene and link they create should show the dramatic action of an event and that the different scenes should move the fairy tale forward. The group may think of each scene and/or link as a curved, straight, fractured, or twisted building block that on the way gets buffeted by events; this means the characters are driven to go forward to escape or change the events. Groups may wish to draw the building blocks and links in their workbook and write in vital scenic information. An example is shown in Figure 8.3.

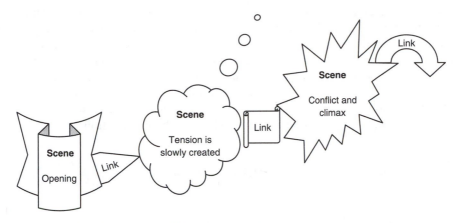

Figure 8.3 Ideas for scenes and links in a fairy tale

The teacher may also ask each group to show the beginning and ending of each scene/ link as this clearly demonstrates if they are creating scenes that move the dramatic action along.

Scenes can be linked by any device, but soundscapes such as the rustle in a forest, a child crying, the donging of a bell can add atmosphere to a fairy tale. These soundscapes can be recorded on a CD and cued to play at the correct moment or they could be created live. Groups could also use atmospheric music to help link their scenes, such as Olivier Messiaen's *Turangalîla-Symphonie* or his *Quartet for the End of Time* or perhaps Jean-Michel Jarre's experimental, instrumental or new age genres.

Phase four: performative phase (about one week)

During this last phase some students may need help to physically and vocally delineate one character from the other. The main problem the playbuilders will come across is that their archetypal characters must have some truth about them although they may verge somewhat on a caricature. To keep changing from one character to another is exciting and challenging but can be taxing, so visually exploring characters can be useful. Students can do this in front of the mirrors in the drama room or at home. They use the mirrors to examine how they are making particular physical changes to improve their trans-formational acting techniques. This activity can be great fun if the class does it together while costumed and made-up.

In this phase the groups continually refine the ways in which the dramatic action, locations and character change in an instant; they explore that the pace of their scenes can be fast and swift or slow and languid, full of menace or joy. Each group will need time on the stage area with the lighting and sound and any other production elements needed. This will most probably require out-of-school rehearsal time. The groups need to make sure they have very simple sets as it is their performing that conveys the locations and the journey of their fairy tale.

It might also be useful for the groups to go back over the quote from their assessment task and ask themselves how they are achieving the essence of this idea as their tales must be full of the marvellous and the horrifying.

These plays are performed to a public audience and the students mingle with their audience afterwards, getting feedback about the different ways they have told stories that stem from a common human experience. This audience feedback should be incorporated into their theatre reviews. The theatre critics should meet a week after the performances giving the students an opportunity to draft and re-draft their work under the guidance of the teacher. The reviews could be pinned around the drama room allowing the class an opportunity to read a variety of them. Using the talking circle the class discuss the reviews, reflect on their own experiences, and evaluate what they have learnt from the project.

Chapter 9

Contemporary classroom playbuilding

This final chapter considers some of the broader issues affecting classroom playbuilding and the shifts in practice that will continue to impact the way playbuilding happens in classrooms. It offers some ideas for playbuilding projects that address these critical issues. Our focus here, as it has been throughout the book, is to help teachers think further about their pedagogy and practice of playbuilding and offer ideas for ways to move these forward.

Looking to the future we know that playbuilders will have many stories to tell and they will tell them in many ways in the classroom. So, in this last exploration of the teaching of playbuilding, we will not provide a single unit of work, rather we will give the teacher a range of ideas to play with as they think and act upon the future of playbuilding in their schools. These ideas are other ways for drama students to engage with this form of learning and complement and contrast the units of work already explored in this book.

SOME RECURRING THEMES

The issues that affect classroom playbuilding at this point in time stem from some of the much broader themes of change and globalisation which impact many fields and spheres of social endeavour such as education, politics, science, technology, cultural work and arts practice. At the beginning of the twenty-first century, notions of art, identity, and community are continually shifting and being stretched in practical, artistic, theoretical and conceptual ways. As a consequence, our current understandings and lived experiences are in flux, in a constant state of becoming. It is difficult to give predictions about what may or may not become of playbuilding practice. What is important is that educators and particularly drama educators consider how these issues affect their work with young people and the kinds of learning experiences that will engage and enrich them in drama and playbuilding. When considering some big picture issues the drama teacher could reflect on the implications of change and contemporary contexts on their teaching of playbuilding, as in the figure below.

Each of these themes have implications for the practice of teaching playbuilding and the types of learning opportunities that can be provided for students. It is important for drama teachers to engage with change and adapt their practice so the classroom work is engaging, innovative and relevant to the worlds students live and create within.

Theme	Questions for reflection
Art	• What constitutes as *art* now? • What are the new forms, ideas and practices? • Who has access? By what means?
Identity	• What discourses, social contexts and practices shape identities, behaviour and their performances (in drama class, in schools, in cultures and communities)? • How does drama help to shape identities? • What types of meanings do students make through their playbuilding projects about selves, others and their worlds? How?
Story	• How do teachers create spaces and processes for effective storying in the drama classroom? • Why is storying important in playbuilding now? • How are stories received, interpreted and represented in playbuilding and what do they reveal about the participants' lives?
Community	• What does it mean to belong? What are the issues? • How do students come to understand and participate in *community* better though their playbuilding projects?
The body	• How are perceptions about bodies changing (in culture, art and in education) and what are the implications for embodied learning in drama and playbuilding? • How do teachers effectively understand and engage students in playbuilding projects that inform understandings and ways of being/using the body?
Place	• Consider experiences and memories of place and space and how these impact and inform both living and playbuilding. • How does students' playbuilding engage with place? In what ways? What are the pedagogical considerations here?
Technology	• How do teachers and students use, learn and engage with and through technologies? • How does technology enhance the playbuilding and the kinds of art works students create? • What possibilities, forms and audiences do technologies open up for student playbuilders and how does the teacher work alongside students as they create in this context? • What are the points of connection and linked processes between immersive technologies and environments and drama learning?

Figure 9.1 Some big picture issues for teacher consideration

PLAYBUILDING WITH A CONTEMPORARY EDGE

Technology-rich playbuilding

It is important to state upfront that we live in a world where technologies are progressing faster than we can write this book! Hence we have not chosen to discuss particular technologies or list software that might indeed be out of date soon after the publication of this text. We are concerned, though, with the pedagogical choices teachers make when using technology to enhance playbuilding projects.

We are defining a technology-rich playbuilding project as one which brings together drama and technology in a variety of ways. This type of playbuilding gives students the opportunity to use multiple forms of information and communication technologies in their units of work. These can be used while creating a play as well as in the play itself, or even as a starting point to playbuild around. The importance of this type of playbuilding is that it is the theatrical meeting point between information and communication technologies and the theatre. Technologies are cross-cultural and this can give a playbuilding project a vision about contemporary life in the global community. It is also a good opportunity to involve a school's information and computer technology department to work in conjunction with the drama department. Students could also research theatre practitioners and companies who use technologies and media in their work, to consider the way contemporary performance is changing and possible techniques they could adapt for their own devising. Whatever the approach taken in technology-rich playbuilding, it is important to experiment with the variety of technological ideas that the students come up with. Often they will know more about the capabilities of modern technologies than the drama teacher, but it is the drama teacher who can help theatricalise this knowledge.

Within technology-rich playbuilding projects teachers should first consider some critical questions to inform their decision making:

- Why use technology?
- When to use technology?
- What types of technologies?
- How to use technologies?

Teachers can sometimes hesitate to use technologies because they can be preoccupied with their own ICT competence (or lack thereof) or they can embrace them haphazardly or superficially without considering fully how they are to use them within the playbuilding process to enhance the learning.

Here are some possible ideas for how technology-rich playbuilding might happen in the drama classroom:

Creating plays that are technology-rich
- Students can explore how video, film, photographs, image, sound, music and lights can help their play be realised with originality and clarity. They can use technology to enhance their stories and create interesting points of emphasis or contrast in their work. This means that the playbuilders will explore the art of looking and the art of seeing, while making meaningful digital image sequences for their work. Students can use technology samples as starting points for playbuilding, for example sms messages, emails or MySpace sites as starting points for devising. Or students can use technology to inject dimensions into the plays they have already begun to devise; perhaps to provide insights into character, or to underscore a piece of live action or to play with dramatic elements such as time or mood. The imagery used could provide a visual through line to their play.

Using technologies for reflection
- Technologies can be used to document the creative process via a series of digital photographs which could then be used as reflective and evaluative teaching and learning tools. Blogs, virtual noticeboards and online forums are interesting ways to

capture student reflection and sharing. Teachers need to establish structures and protocols for students to use these effectively. Teachers also need to have ways of monitoring such tools, so that they provide rich learning opportunities rather than superficial ways for students to engage with the work.

Using the internet within the playbuilding itself

- Using the theme of technology as a starting point students could playbuild around the rapidly changing computerised world in which they live, allowing them to reappraise their frames of reference and where the internet or part of this phenomenon is the actual story and is live on stage. For example, the set and the story could be intertwined, the set being made up of a central performance area surrounded by computer monitors that show the devised play in real time, as well as at other times showing documentary videos that can create an alternative to the meaning of the play. Also there could be live internet connections that are manipulated by the characters and the audience at certain pivotal moments in the play (Kennedy and Lovesy 1997).

Cyber-playbuilding: creating and sharing practice online

- Cyber-playbuilding is where playbuilders go online to devise plays with other schools. This type of playbuilding is created in the classroom online or pre-recorded and is transmitted to another school's playbuilding classroom taking into account different time zones. A school's drama department contacts another school's drama department which is in a near or faraway location, and sets up an online playbuilding project where there is an exchange of process and performances via live or pre-recorded video of a joint playbuilding project. This can be through vodcasting or they can even share materials through other virtual or more immersive spaces that could be constructed for learning purposes by the schools. Perhaps the devised work could link thematically or each scene could be the starting point for the other school to work from. There is a multitude of ways the work could be shared and used to generate insights but also feed into the playbuilding process itself.

- The teachers from both schools would have to agree what the principles of this cyberspace meeting and performing zone are before and during the teaching of this project. They would consider and plan such things as:

  ○ The safety and organisational requirements to be implemented before the project starts and as the project continues; for example timelines and time zones, technological requirements, interpersonal relationships and student safety in cyberspace.

  ○ What the similarities and differences are in their pedagogic teaching approach to playbuilding.

  ○ How will the playbuilders initially interact with one another to break down any barriers that might exist; for example using free software that allows the playbuilders to communicate with other playbuilders around the world via audio and video links.

  ○ Will the two playbuilding classes be devising different playbuilding projects and sharing their experiences about the process and performances? Will they take a similar starting point and then reflect and evaluate why the projects took different dramatic paths? What are the different social or cultural ideas that emerge in the storytelling?

  ○ Will the two playbuilding classes devise one playbuilding project between them?

> If this is the case perhaps scenes are developed and pre-recorded in the classroom, or online, and then put together via relevant software for a final performance through live and recorded moments.
>
> ○ Organising for the playbuilders to meet in person during or after the project, for example at a weekend playbuilding excursion, or at a national or international drama conference.

Technology-rich playbuilding opens up a myriad of new ways for playbuilders to tell their stories as it creates the learning environment for students to use and value the technological diversity of the global society in which they live.

Body-centred playbuilding

In performance and theatre, there has been an expansion of interest and practice in the arts with a focus on the body. In a body-centred playbuilding project, students explore physical and visual communications to generate their play, primarily using the body to tell a visual story. It can be thought of as a response to speech-based or word entrenched theatre as it engages in the universal languages of mime, movement, dance, physical theatre, music and sound. This type of playbuilding operates very much in students' personal body space, and this space can be called their personal kinesphere (Newlove 1993). Through this way of devising, students are connecting to, and overlapping with, other students' kinespheres. They pass through the space using their physical and visual abilities, engaging with their imaginations through creating body and sound metaphors and a playbuilder's kinaesthetic language occurs spontaneously on the classroom floor through their bodily kinaesthetic intelligence. The often limited verbal content of body-centred playbuilding can be most challenging to some playbuilders as they have to work in new ways such as physically clarifying mood, symbols, and dramatic meaning to get their play's story across to their audience. It is also important to remember that some students are not as confident in bodily movement work as others, and their needs must also be catered for and so it is very important for the teacher to spend time encouraging every group's creativity and physical expressions.

In a classroom project where the focus of the unit of work is on exploring physical ways of telling a story with limited dialogue, the playbuilders could experiment with neutral masks, music, and tangible or imagined drama properties. They could also use a non-linear scene structure and draw on the performance style of the surreal if appropriate. Physical improvisation activities are important in this type of project and they could include the whole class simultaneously offering and accepting abstract ideas such as responding to words that they can create shapes to, or phrases that involve them exploring rhythmic actions. These types of improvisations can carry an implicit sense of drama and theatre within them, suggesting to playbuilders that there is a movement-based opening for them in which to participate at whatever level matches their ability.

To begin the generative phase it would be wise to ask the playbuilders how they see this type of playbuilding in contrast to their other playbuilding projects, or even their scripted drama projects, and what they see as the pros and cons of working in this way. From these discussions improvisation groups of two, three, and four can be quickly formed and dispersed using the students' bodily kinaesthetic intuition. For example, the class is asked to mill around the room, not talking to one another but engaging with the imagery and sounds that suggest the feeling, or impulse, of a starting point such as *The Dream*. Students become:

In a group of two:

- the exact, then exaggerated, shadow of their partner.

In a group of three:

- light and darkness.

In a group of four:

- a swirling nightmare
- A tingling dream.

This type of improvisation is a potent means for the playbuilders to safely explore creative movement and to establish a physical basis for their future storytelling.

In the constructing phase improvisation activities could be a base and an inspiration to help each group create a storyline and to help them find and establish a motif before they start to construct abstract scenes that will be linked together later in the process. In phase three structuring, the groups could explore and add neutral masks, and then extend the stylistic aspects of their physical storytelling by adding sudden, strong or automated movement, or flexible, sustained and light movements attempting to clarify how their body-based scenes are progressing before moving on. In phase four performative, the teacher would need to provide refinement teaching strategies that have a strong kinaesthetic connection to their playbuilders' body-based play, such as running scenes with limited dialogue, and then with no dialogue, and experimenting with music and sound or movement patterns that are allied to breath and voice, so that the visual story becomes clearer and more powerful for their potential audience.

Body-centred playbuilding can be very exciting to teach but because of the complexity for some students, who are at times unsure of their bodies, let alone of thinking about the dynamic of how a story can be reflected through their bodies, playbuilding performances may only be two to four minutes long and as playbuilders' skills progress more challenging times may be achieved.

Body-centred playbuilding gives playbuilders an opportunity to use all or part of their bodies to construct stories and to reflect and evaluate how they have connected their bodies and minds to create dramatic meaning for their audience.

FINAL THOUGHTS . . .

Young at Art is a book that explores the dynamic and imaginative world of playbuilding. We believe that the ideas presented in this book open up a myriad of creative possibilities in the drama learning space, enabling playbuilders to devise their own unique and diverse plays. We would like to stress that the very unique nature of playbuilding necessitates a high level of trust between participants (Arnold 1993); this is because of the very special personal and imaginative creating that occurs.

Teaching in a sensitive, constructive and empathic manner is an effective way of helping the groups to release their imaginations while engaging in the playbuilding processes. Teaching in this mode means that the drama teacher creates vibrant playbuilding learning within their own drama syllabus framework. When the drama teacher facilitates the dynamic between affect, cognition and physicality in their teaching they are creating a mode of learning where their playbuilders gain licence to become excited and exhilarated, as well as understanding that the unknown and the disconcerting are part of this drama learning process.

As the drama teacher you will be genuinely startled, surprised, delighted and confronted by the ideas your playbuilders come up with; this means that your playbuilding groups are testing, rearranging and shifting through the rhythms of their group's imagination to explore their perceptions of the world.

Playbuilding has the extraordinary potential to help students to explore and transform their own and their group's ideas, thus allowing all playbuilders to contemplate and devise plays that pose and solve human problems. In this sense, playbuilding becomes a process where important meaning making takes place, as students learn to create and collaborate to devise their own unique works. Playbuilding places the students and their creativity central in the learning process and offers safe spaces and structured processes for humanity and imagination to flourish. It is a form of drama learning that engages young people in dynamic ways by inviting them to investigate their worlds, manipulate the symbolic elements of the art form and work together to communicate their own ideas and engage their audiences. Students may be young at art and at life but through the devising process they can learn valuable skills and understandings that last well beyond the drama classroom.

References

Appel, L. 1982, *Mask Characterization: An Acting Process*, Southern Illinois University Press, Illinois.

Arnold, R. 1993, 'The Nature and Role of Empathy in Human Development and in Drama Education', in W. Michaels (ed.), *Drama in Education: The State of the Art II*, Educational Drama Association NSW, Sydney.

Arnold, R. 2005, *Empathic Intelligence: Teaching, Learning, Relating*, University of New South Wales Press, Australia.

Berry, K. 2000, *The Dramatic Arts and Cultural Studies*, Falmer Press, New York.

Blom, L. A., and Chaplin, L. T. 1988, *The Moment of Movement: Dance Improvisation*, University of Pittsburgh Press, Pittsburgh, Pa.

Boal, A. 1995, *Rainbow of Desire*, trans. A. Jackson, Routledge, London.

Bolton, G. 1979, *Towards a Theory of Drama in Education*, Longman, Essex.

Bolton, G. 1986, in D. Davis and C. Lawrence (eds), *Gavin Bolton: Selected Writings on Drama in Education*, Longman, London.

Bolton, G. 1992, *New Perspectives on Classroom Drama*, Simon and Schuster, Hemel Hempstead.

Brecht, B. 1996, *Mother Courage and Her Children*, adapted by D. Hare, Arcade Publishing, New York.

Burton, B. 1991, *The Act of Learning: The Drama-Theatre Continuum in the Classroom*, Longman Cheshire, South Melbourne.

Canton, K. 1994, *The Fairy Tale Revisited*, Peter Lang, New York.

Carroll, J. 1988, 'Terra Incognita: Mapping Drama Talk', *NJ Drama Australia Journal*, vol. 12, no. 2, pp.13–21.

Carroll, J. 1996, 'Escaping the Information Abattoir: Critical and Transformative Research in Drama Classrooms', in P. Taylor (ed.), *Researching Drama and Arts Education*, Falmer Press, London.

Coult, T. and Kershaw, B. (eds) 1999, *Engineers of the Imagination: The Welfare State Handbook*, rev edn, Methuen, London.

Fox, J. 2002, *Eyes on Stalks*, Methuen, London.

Friel, B. 1990, *Dancing at Lughnasa*, Faber and Faber, London.

Friel, B. 1999, in *Brian Friel: Essays, Diaries, Interviews 1964–1999*, ed. C. Murray, Faber and Faber, London.

Gallagher, K. 2007, *Theatre of Urban: Schooling in Dangerous Times*, University of Toronto Press, Toronto.

Gardner, H. 1993, *Multiple Intelligences: The Theory in Practice*, Basic Books, New York.

Goodwin, J. 1989, *British Theatre Design: The Modern Age*, St Martin's Press, New York.

Greig, A. 2005, *Playwriting: A Practical Guide*, Routledge, London.

Hardy, B. 1968, 'Towards a Poetics of Fiction: An Approach through Narrative', *Novel*, vol. 2, pp. 5–14.

Haseman, B. and O'Toole, J. 1986, *Dramawise*, Heinemann Educational Australia, Port Melbourne, Victoria.

Haseman, B. 2002, 'The "Leaderly" Process Drama and the Artistry of "Rip Mix and Burn" ', in B. Rasmussen and A.L. Ostern (eds), *Playing Betwixt and Between: The IDEA Dialogues 2001*, IDEA Publications, Bergen.

Hatton, C. 2001, 'A Girls' Own Project: Subjectivity and Transformation in Girls' Drama', *NJ, Drama Australia Journal*, vol. 25, no. 1, pp. 21–30.

Hatton, C. 2002, 'Staging the Subjective: A Narrative Approach to Drama', in *NJ Drama Australia Journal: Selected Papers IDEA 2001*, vol. 26, no. 1, pp. 81–8.

Hatton, C. 2003, 'Backyards and Borderlands: Some Reflections on Researching the Travels of Adolescent Girls Doing Drama' (extended version), in *Research in Drama Education*, vol. 8, no. 2, pp. 139–56.

Hatton, C. 2004a, 'Backyards and Borderlands: Transforming Girls Learning through Drama', unpublished doctoral thesis, University of Sydney.

Hatton, C. 2004b, 'On the Edge of Realities: Drama Learning and Adolescent Girls', in *NJ Drama Australia Journal*, vol. 28, no. 1, pp. 87–103.

Hatton, C. 2004c, 'Exploring the "Potential Space" of drama in the Secondary Classroom', in C. Hatton and M. Anderson (eds), *The State of Our Art: NSW Perspectives in Drama Education*, Currency Press, Sydney.

Hatton, C. 2006, 'Can I Get a Witness? Mapping Learning in and beyond the Drama Classroom?', in *Journal of Creative and Artistic Education*, vol. 1, no. 1, pp. 171–204.

Heddon, D. and Milling, J. 2006, *Devising Performance: A Critical History*, Palgrave Macmillan, Basingstoke.

Holder, J. 1982, 'The Loner', in J. Foster (ed.), *A Third Poetry Book*, Oxford University Press, Oxford.

Kennedy, P., and Lovesy, S. 1997, 'Political Playbuilding for Senior Students', paper presented at the 8th International Conference for the Asian Pacific Confederation for Arts Education July, University of Melbourne.

Kristeva, J. 1981, 'Women's Time', in *Signs*, vol. 7, no. 1, pp. 5–12.

Lemasson, S. 1999, 'Devising through Improvisation: The Construction Site', in D. Williams (ed.), *Collaborative Theatre: The Théâtre du Soleil Sourcebook*, Routledge, London.

Lovesy, S. 2002, 'Performing an Essay', in *NJ Drama Australia Journal*, vol. 26, no. 2, pp. 83–91.

Lovesy, S. 2003, 'Drama Education Secondary School Playbuilding', unpublished doctoral thesis, University of Western Sydney, Sydney, New South Wales, Australia.

Lovesy, S.C. 2005a, 'Identification of Gifted and Talented Drama Students', in *Drama NSW Big Book of Ideas*, Drama NSW & Australian Government Quality Teacher Programme Publication, Sydney.

Lovesy, S.C. 2005b, 'Performing an Essay', in *Drama NSW Big Book of Ideas: Australian Government Quality Teacher Programme*, Drama NSW & Australian Government Quality Teacher Programme Publication, Sydney.

McAdams, D. 1993, *The Stories We Live By: Personal Myths and the Making of the Self*, William Morrow and Company, New York.

Merlin, B. 2003, *Konstantin Stanislavsky: Routledge Performance Practitioners*, Routledge, London.

Miller, J. 2007, *Ariane Mnouchkine: Routledge Performance Practitioners*, Routledge, London.

Moore, C.-L., and Yamamoto, K. 1988, *Beyond Words: Movement Observation and Analysis*, Gordon and Breach, New York.

Morgan, N. and Saxton, J. 1994, *Asking Better Questions*, Pembroke, Ontario.

Murray, J. H. 1997, *Hamlet on the Holodeck: The Future of Narrative in Cyberspace*, Free Press, New York.

Murray, S. 2003, *Jacques Lecoq: Routledge Performance Practitioners*, Routledge, London.

Needlands, J. and Goode, T. 1990, *Structuring Drama Work*, Cambridge University Press, Cambridge.

Newlove, J. 1993, *Laban for Actors and Dancers: Putting Laban's Movement Theory into Practice*, Routledge, New York.

Noddings, N. 1984, *Caring: A Feminine Approach to Ethics and Moral Education*, University of California Press, Berkeley and Los Angeles.

Noddings, N. and Witherell, C. 1991, *Stories Lives Tell*, Teachers' College Press, New York.

Oddey, A. 1994, *Devising Theatre*, Routledge, London.

O'Toole, J. 1992, *The Process of Drama: Negotiating Art and Meaning*, Routledge, London.

Polkinghorne, D. 1988, *Narrative Knowing and the Human Sciences*, State University of New York Press, New York.

Pór, G. (Compiled by), 2006, *Talking Stick Circle: An Ancient Tool for Better Decision Making and Strengthening Community*. Retrieved June 13, 2006 from <www.vision-nest.com/btbc/kgarden/tscicle.shtml>.

Print, M. 1993, *Curriculum Development and Design*, Allen and Unwin, St Leonards, Australia.

Propp, V. 1984, in A.Y. Martin and R.P. Martin (eds), *Theory and History of Folklore*, trans; A. Liberman, University of Minnesota Press, Minneapolis.

Sallis, R. 2004, 'Con and Charlie Do the Splits: Multiple Masculinities and Drama Pedagogy', in *NJ Drama Australia Journal*, vol. 28, no. 1, pp.104–17.

Simons, J. 1997, 'Drama, Pedagogy and the Art of Double Meaning', *Research in Drama Education*, vol. 2, no. 2, pp.193–201

Thomson, P. 1997, *Brecht: Mother Courage and Her Children: Plays in Production*, Cambridge University Press, Cambridge.

Tolkien, J.R.R. 1983/2006, 'On Fairy Stories', in C. Tolkien (ed.), *The Monsters and the Critics: And Other Essays*, HarperCollins Publishers, London.

Vygotsky, L. 1978, in V. John-Steiner, S. Schribner and E. Souberman (eds), *Mind in Society*, trans. M. Cole, Harvard University Press, Cambridge, MA.

Weigler, W. 2001, *Strategies for Playbuilding*, Heinemann, Portsmouth, NH.

Wiggins, G. and McTighe, J. 2001, *Understanding by Design*, Prentice-Hall Inc, USA.

Willett, J. 1964, *Brecht on Theatre*, trans. J. Willett, Methuen, London.

Williams, D. (ed.) 1999, *Collaborative Theatre: The Théâtre du Soleil Sourcebook*, Routledge, London.

Yakim, M. and Broadman, M. 1990, *Creating a Character: A Physical Approach to Acting*, Applause, New York.

Zatzman, B. 2003, 'The Monologue Project: Drama as a Form of Witnessing', in K. Gallagher and D. Booth (eds), *How Theatre Educates: Convergences and Counterpoints*, University of Toronto Press, Toronto.

Drama syllabuses and curriculum frameworks cited

NSW Office of the Board of Studies, Australia, *Stage 6 Drama Syllabus* 1992.

Ministry of Education, Province of British Columbia, Canada, *Drama Resource Packages* 1955 and 2002.

New York State Education Department, USA, *Theatre: A Resource Guide for Standards-Based Instruction*, November 2004.

Index

eBooks

eBooks – at www.eBookstore.tandf.co.uk

A library at your fingertips!

eBooks are electronic versions of printed books. You can store them on your PC/laptop or browse them online.

They have advantages for anyone needing rapid access to a wide variety of published, copyright information.

eBooks can help your research by enabling you to bookmark chapters, annotate text and use instant searches to find specific words or phrases. Several eBook files would fit on even a small laptop or PDA.

NEW: Save money by eSubscribing: cheap, online access to any eBook for as long as you need it.

Annual subscription packages

We now offer special low-cost bulk subscriptions to packages of eBooks in certain subject areas. These are available to libraries or to individuals.

For more information please contact webmaster.ebooks@tandf.co.uk

We're continually developing the eBook concept, so keep up to date by visiting the website.

www.eBookstore.tandf.co.uk